APPLE

Learning to Design, Designing to Learn

Ken Miki

Lars Müller Publishers

What does it mean to think, make, convey, and learn?

APPLE

Learning to Design, Designing to Learn

Ken Miki

Preface

01 | Apple: Observation—Breakdown

02 | Apple: Observation—Length

03 | Apple: Observation—Area

04 | Apple: Observation—Color

Preface

For those who are studying design for the first time,
those who have been involved with design for many years,
those who are teaching design,
and those who have no interest in design

On an important milestone in my career, the thirtieth anniversary of my design firm, Ken Miki & Associates, I accepted a teaching position in the Design Department at Osaka University of Arts. What kind of training could I provide to these young people poised to enter the world of design? I was asked to oversee a freshman course in basic design practice. After approaching design from a variety of angles during the first year, they would begin to concentrate on a specialty as sophomores. Not all of them, however, were aiming to become designers in the future.

In this book, I lay out the educational method I developed as basic practice for those studying design for the first time. Using an apple, something familiar to everyone, to help convey the true nature of design, I devised a program divided into sections dealing with various concepts that would cultivate insight through the following keywords: thinking, making, conveying, and learning. This book is intended for those who are studying design for the first time, those who have been involved with design for many years, those who are teaching design, and those who have no interest in design

Design has been closely linked to our lives and society for ages, but there is still a common misconception that design refers to superficial colors or a kind of veneer. As suggested by Steve Jobs' comment that "design is not what it looks like," there is more to design than mere ornamentation. The word "design" is derived from the French *dessin* (drawing), which can in turn be traced to the Latin *designare*, meaning "to mark out a plan." Today, the word design is used as a concept that not only expresses a medium or product but also the creation of a mechanism. Design has been described as the act of making a smooth connection between people, people and tangible things, or people and intangible things through communication by identifying a certain state of mind or set of circumstances. Thus, in addition to traversing a professional field, design necessarily embodies a rich sustainable life.

In other words, design visualizes ideas and concepts that provide solutions to a variety of problems. This calls for the discovery of social themes and a special sense of awareness to covert them into new values. And attaining this level of awareness requires profound insight.

This program was conceived to help students understand the essential nature of design through the following six-step process: understanding, observation, imagination, analysis, revision, and visualization. First, it is important to accurately "understand" the theme. Limited by preconceptions and prejudices, many of us fail to correctly identify the reasons, causes, and significance of the matter at hand. We have a vague notion of something without thoroughly understanding it. Or more to the point, many of us do not realize that we do not understand. Understanding is the door to everything else. Next, it is important to steadily "observe" our subject by searching for its source, determining relationships, and accumulating facts. This is what it means to observe. Then, deriving a concept from this information, we begin to construct an idea in three dimensions as if we were erecting a building based on our objective. In this "imaginative" act, we build up a hypothesis. Next, it is vital to find a necessity in the concept that links the subject to our objectives. Once the necessity becomes clear, we have to "analyze" it. Unless we have the courage to analyze and restructure our plan, we will simply continue to move forward without taking note of various disparities that have arisen. In some cases, this leads to an irrevocable failure from which there is no return. Now it is time to "revise"—and turn our plan into a narrative. This involves deriving a concept based on a unique perspective, defining clear content, and determining a course of activity. All of the principles and concepts needed to take concrete action are now in place. We have reached the final step: visualization. It is sometimes said that design is the act of expressing a principle in an easy-to-understand and original way. Thus, we might see design as a child born of principle. Each of these steps helps us attain an awareness of new values and ideas. It is this process that gives birth to design.

Discovering Your Own Way of Living

For those studying design for the first time, what I have to convey will probably gradually become clear. At this point, I would like to state my objectives in this course. Through each research task, you will achieve a better understanding of the essential nature of design through the experiences of thinking, making, conveying, and learning. What does it mean to think? It means to recognize the importance of concepts that underlie our thinking such as organizing information, generating content, evolving ideas, and performing revisions. What does it mean to make? It means to search for a unique way of creating something based on ideas such as observing, making rules, deleting names, and making names without being constrained by existing rules or tools. What does it mean to convey? It means to form bonds with people and society through acts of communication or facilitation such as understanding other people's ideas, designing as if you were talking, devising a comprehensible approach, and broadening your sympathies. What does it mean to learn? It means to find something worth doing in circumstances that involve influence, torment, and sharing, conjuring up enough gumption to inspire yourself, and developing the ability to understand what you want to learn. Think logically. Open up your senses. Constantly moving back and forth between your intellect and sensitivity is what makes design attractive and enjoyable. These are my main objectives in this course. We are constantly faced with a variety of situations that call for questioning in regard to thinking, making, conveying, and learning. Or to put it a different way, rather than being satisfied with the things we have or striving for more, the real question is how to discover our own way of living. This is what I want to convey to my students.

Why an Apple?

Next, I would like to touch on the reason that I chose apples as the basis for this course.

My goal was to create an accessible workshop that would help you understand the essential nature of design by the end of this fifteen-week course. This required content that would get to the heart of design rather than only skimming the surface. I thought that using something familiar to everyone in the world might lead to deeper understanding. "What kind of subject would allow people to perceive information using all five of their senses?" Then I suddenly noticed the apple I was eating for breakfast. Apples are connected to everything—seeing, hearing, feeling, smelling, and tasting. And I thought that by the end of each class, you would be able to digest the content in exactly the same way that you eat an apple. By doing this, I thought I could give "awareness" a physical form. But more than that, by choosing an apple, I thought I could make this a "delicious" class. *Oishii*, the Japanese word for "delicious," is derived from *ishi*, written with the *kanji* character for "beauty." From the early twelfth to the mid-sixteenth century during the Kamakura and Muromachi Periods, *ishi* meant "good," "pleasant," "splendid," "clever," and "tasty." The characters used to write *oishii* (delicious) were simply chosen as phonetic equivalents, but they mean "beautiful" and "taste." Beauty is an indispensable part of design. Taste is an indispensable part

of an apple. Besides being one of the five senses, the word "taste" is sometimes used to express elegance in phrases like "good taste" or "tasteful." The *kanji* for "taste" is also included in compounds like *imi* ("meaning"). "Meaning" refers to the content, concept, proposition or intention expressed by a word. Though "meaning" is a straightforward English translation of *imi*, we might also say "concept." A sense of beauty and a concept are essential in determining the nature of design. Then I started to wonder how I could express meanings like "things gained from experience" and "the charm of a thing," which are also contained in the word *aji*. I decided that the English word "appreciate" (as in "art appreciation") was quite close. "Appreciate" means to "savor," "recognize the quality of," "perceive," and "show gratitude for." Recognizing the quality of something is also related to understanding, perceiving is connected to observation, and gratitude is a fundamental attitude in learning. This convinced me that the apple was the perfect material.

Turning to the wider world, we find that apples played a central role in many inventions, discoveries, and creations throughout history. The forbidden fruit that Adam and Eve ate was an apple. Isaac Newton discovered the law of universal gravitation with an apple. The Beatles, who drove the world mad with their music, started Apple Records. And Steve Jobs created a computer revolution with a company called Apple. It was as if the God of Design had commanded me to use apples. And this is how I arrived at my basic approach for this course.

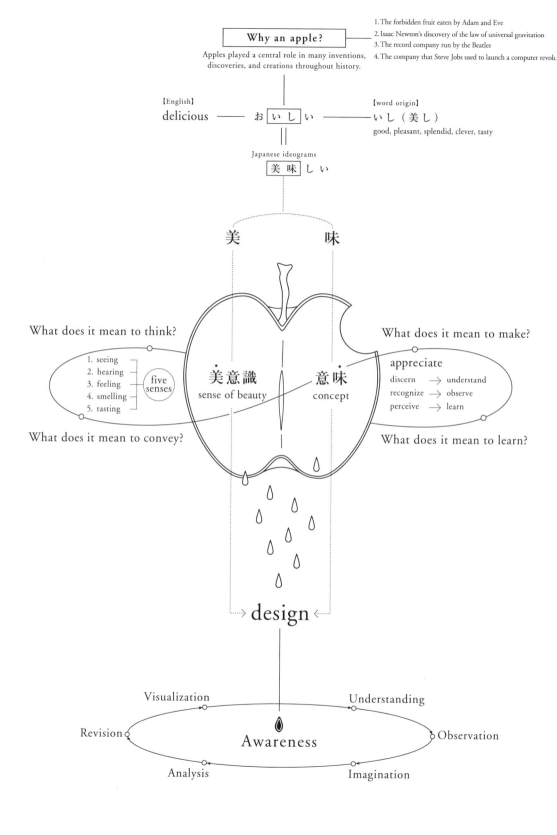

Why an apple?

Apples played a central role in many inventions, discoveries, and creations throughout history.

1. The forbidden fruit eaten by Adam and Eve
2. Isaac Newton's discovery of the law of universal gravitation
3. The record company run by the Beatles
4. The company that Steve Jobs used to launch a computer revolu...

【English】
delicious —— お い し い —— いし（美し）
good, pleasant, splendid, clever, tasty

【word origin】

Japanese ideograms
美 味 し い

美　味

What does it mean to think?

1. seeing
2. hearing
3. feeling
4. smelling
5. tasting

five senses

美意識
sense of beauty

意味
concept

What does it mean to make?

appreciate

discern → understand
recognize → observe
perceive → learn

What does it mean to convey?

What does it mean to learn?

design

Visualization　Understanding

Revision　Awareness　Observation

Analysis　Imagination

01 | Apple : Observation—Breakdown

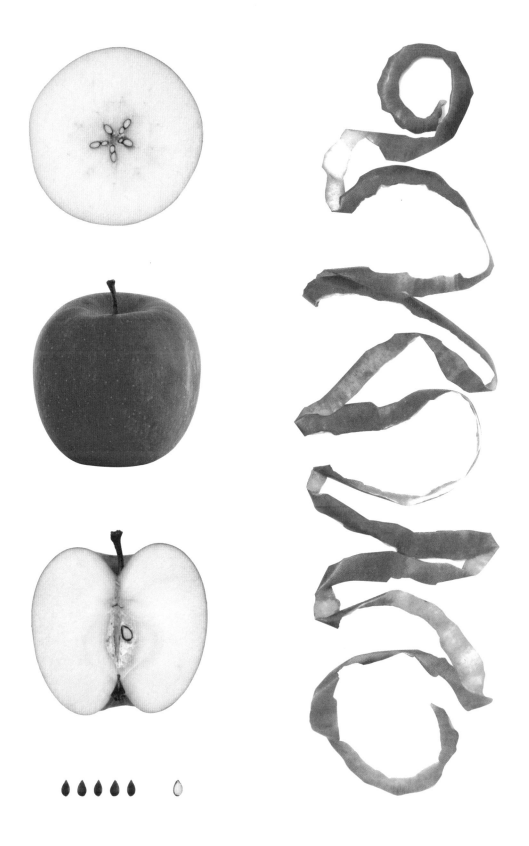

The Fruit You Thought You Knew

When did you first eat an apple? Did your mother grate it and feed it to you as a baby? When did you first touch an apple? Was it on a shopping trip to the fruit shop? When did you first peel an apple? Was it when you were helping your mother in the kitchen? Almost immediately after we are born, we come into repeated contact with apples.

If someone asked you to verbalize an apple, the most common response would probably be "red, round, and delicious." If someone asked you to draw an apple, most people would make a red or green, round or heart-shaped object. Despite having savored apples with all of our senses (seeing, hearing, feeling, smelling, and tasting) since we were children, our awareness of them is extremely limited. Why? The answer lies in the difference between perception and recognition. The apple in our memory is the embodiment of a vague perception that most of us have maintained for a long period of time. To accurately comprehend something, we must call it into our consciousness by assigning meaning to the information we obtained through our perceptions. Thus, perception does not necessarily mean recognition. There is a difference, that is, between looking and seeing. Recognition is something we can objectively verify through output such as actions or spoken utterances. Depicting a subject through a sketch or drawing is not merely a means of copying the thing. It is a way of deepening our awareness of the subject while gazing at the parts and the

whole. In the process of posing questions to ourselves, we observe the subject as we verbalize it, and output the information in the form of a picture. Through visualization and verbalization, we deepen our recognition. Through perception, we believe we understand something.

I Saw the Same Thing, But It Was Different

You sometimes see the owner of a fruit shop tapping an apple and recommending it to a customer, "This one is really fresh!" A high, clear sound is proof that the fruit is fresh, and a low, muddy sound shows that it is ripe. It is also said that apples that feel heavy, have a good coloring that extends all the way to the bottom, and a deep depression in the blossom end are fresh and tasty. Like a doctor examining a patient with her stethoscope, we can diagnose the condition of an apple based on its sound, weight, color, and shape. "Observation" is the act of carefully looking at something to understand its true state. We examine its appearance and record any changes that might occur. The degree of change that you can detect is also important. Observation can be broadly divided into two categories: quantitative and qualitative.

Quantitative observation involves focusing on continuous numeric change in the state of a subject. In physical and natural science, research is primarily based on a logical explanation of a phenomenon through the use

of a formula. This allows us to explain the subject quantitatively. On the other hand, qualitative observation involves focusing on discontinuous change in the nature of a subject. In sociology and cultural anthropology, research is primarily based on qualitative aspects such as interviews, survey results, texts, films, and historical records. In other words, a subject can be analyzed both quantitatively and qualitatively. These two methods allow us to observe an apple. The important thing is what we notice in the process. Some people believe that observation involves collecting documents and keeping records. But the most crucial aspect is the way in which we interpret this information.

In this program, our main goal is not to make quantitative observations based on scientific values. Rather, it is our job to come up with the simplest method of measurement possible. In other words, we should consider how to measure and then use our bodies to confront the apple. We can start by breaking the apple down by measuring its surface area and indicating the length of its circumference. This is apt to lead to an astonishing discovery. A discovery is a "realization." It deepens our curiosity and strengthens our interest in the subject. Though we are all looking at the same thing, each of us sees something different. This is a clear manifestation of the difference between perception and recognition.

Becoming the World's Greatest Researcher

This research project is focused entirely on examining the essential nature of design through an apple. By expanding our interest to include various aspects of the apple world, we come into contact with nearly every corner of society. What kind of water and soil are needed to grow apples? How have apples been affected by global warming? What does the future hold for apple farmers in light of current trade issues? What route is used to transport apples to the market? How will apple farmers be able to carry on their business with so few successors? Through questions like these, we become aware of a variety of environmental, international, economic, distributive, and personnel problems. In attempting to investigate something, all sorts of links become apparent. The world is all connected. We might choose to think global and act local, or think local and act global. Combining these two strategies has also led to the coinage of a new word: "glocal". This is my message to you. The world expands through the differences between perception and recognition. I hope you will follow the subtitle of this workshop and become the world's greatest researcher.

02 | Apple: Observation—Length

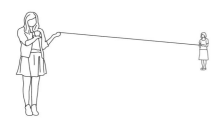

Subtracting Information

"How could we simply measure the circumference of an organic form like an apple? And how we could we make a measuring tool out of everyday items without relying on any special instruments?" One student raised her hand and suggested that we might wind a piece of string around the apple and then measure its length. My questions were meant to inspire a flexible notion that corresponds to the circumstances; I was looking for a kind of "living wisdom." I also wanted my students to become more aware of the "process of making" by encouraging them to create or discover a measuring tool. Just as an artisan makes a tool to fit his particular needs, you can come up with a device when what you have been given does not quite work. It is necessary to realize something that is useful, effective, and beautiful; and a tool based on a streamlined concept will enrich your expression.

The students started by preparing four colors (red, green, black, and white) of 2 mm wide cord to wrap around the apples, some of which were red and some green. Then, they completely covered the surface of the apples with double-sided tape. Next, they wound the red cords around the red apples, and the green cords around the green apples. The black and white cords could be used for either kind. The important thing was to carefully wind the cord so that it fit tightly around the apple. Even the smallest amount of slack would be impossible to fix and would force

the students to repeat the process all over again. After they had finished winding the cords, some of the female students exclaimed, "How cute!" Others said that the ones with black cords looked like they had had a magic spell cast on them or that they looked cool. Stories related to apples and flashes of intuition had instantly sparked their imagination. Each apple contained a poetic metaphor. Next, they observed the apples, which were now objects. They looked at them from the side, from above, and went through various stages. And they began to realize how distorted apples are, and how much their shapes differ from one to another. By replacing the information contained in the object with the color and material of the cord, they were able to see things that they had never seen before. By subtracting information, they also understood how complex and varied the information contained in an apple could be. The difference between "perception" and "recognition" had suddenly become very clear.

A Fusion of Functional Beauty and Emotional Beauty

The apple's distorted form was manifested by the cord, which transformed it into an object. By reexamining natural objects in our surroundings, we find that many of them are organically distorted. People are no different. At first glance, our faces and bodies seem to be symmetrical, but if you folded them in half, you would find that the two parts are not completely equal. And among our organs, the heart, stomach,

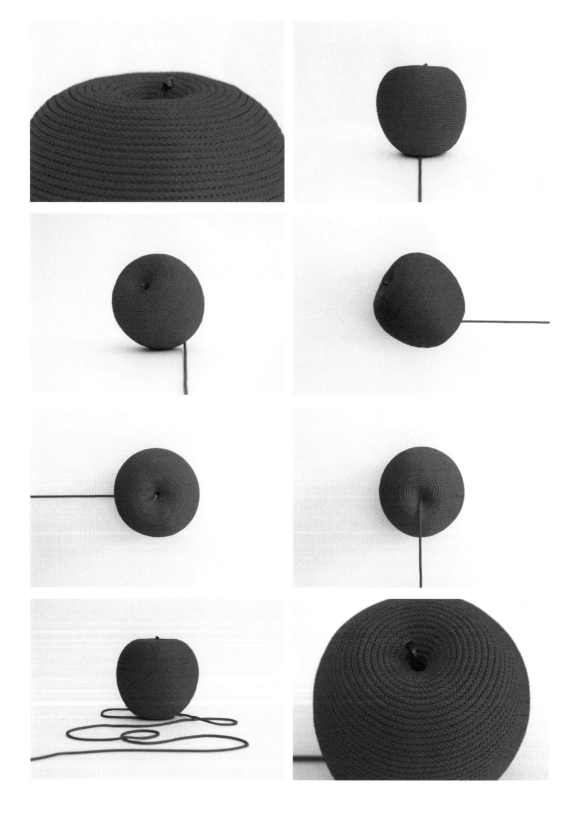

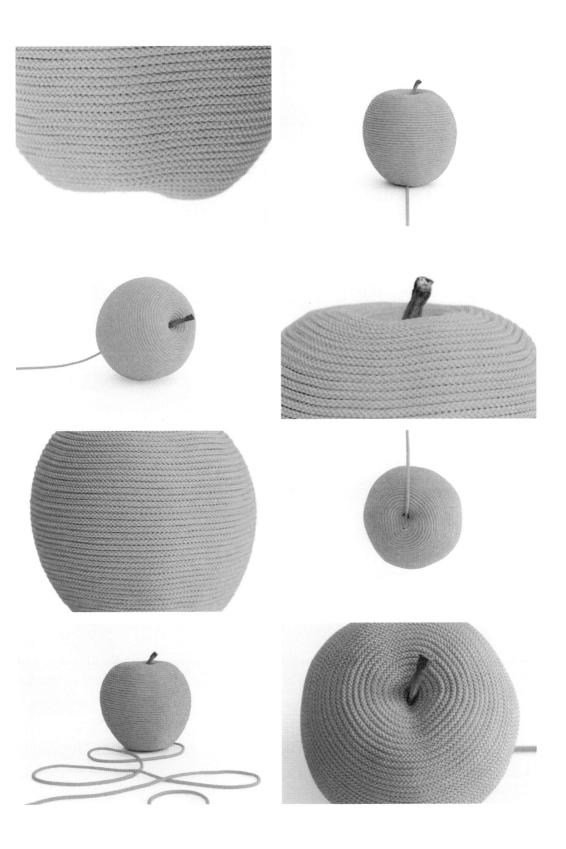

and intestines are particularly asymmetrical. Made up of the prefix "sym-," meaning "to unify," and the suffix "-metry," meaning "measurement," the word "symmetry" signifies a state of "balance" and "harmony."

Why do people make things that are symmetrical? Perhaps it is because the stylistic beauty of symmetry is an imaginary state that we aspire to as creatures that are not completely symmetrical. Assuming this is true, we might then say that we are searching for a stable sense of harmony in the countless examples of symmetry that can be found in architecture, painting, and various ornaments. A quick look at the implements we use in daily life also reveals a host of symmetrical designs, such as tables, chairs, spoons, dishes, notebooks, and pencils. In this case, the search for functional beauty led to the symmetrical form. If a baseball and a bat were not symmetrical, the ball would soar in some unpredictable direction when it was hit. It might be interesting to create a new game in which we could enjoy an irregular succession of things, but this approach would not be suitable for household items or sports equipment. Tools are followed by a distinct function.

On the other hand, our inner nature also tends to be organically deformed. When we consider communication and community design, it is necessary to devise a flexible concept along with an organic sensation such as the cord we used to measure the apples. People are moved and saddened by trivial things. Our facial expressions and physical behaviors are likely to be influenced by our emotions. The thing that makes a painting, book or movie enchanting is its emotional beauty. Our heart often beats faster, throbs or flutters for illogical things. Love is one example. We are often driven by something illogical. By fusing functional beauty and emotional beauty, we set out to find a sense of "satisfaction."

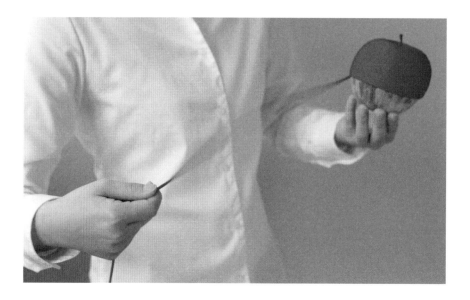

Transience, Sorrow, and Gallantry

Just after the students finished observing the cord-covered apples, I instructed them to undo the cords in one go. This prompted plaintive sighs from some of them. Although the original goal had been to measure the apples' circumference, many of them were absorbed in its altered form. The sense of accomplishment that arose from covering the apples with cords and transforming them into beautiful objects had caused them to lose sight of the goal. But if they just left the apples as they were, they would eventually rot. Everything alive must at some time die. Through this truth, we become acquainted with a sense of transience and sorrow. I think Japanese people like cherry blossoms for their neat beauty, short life span, and also because they are captivated by the lovely dance of the petals—a kind of visualization of the wind's movement—when they are scattered. Perhaps we sense a kind of gallant beauty in things that vanish in a faint, fragile, or simple way that we associate with transience and sorrow. The reason I asked the students to undo the cords in one go was to make them aware of this kind of transience or the "quickness" of design. By "quickness," I mean a sense of "resolve" or "decisiveness." Design does not incorporate every kind of information. It requires the ability to assess what should remain.

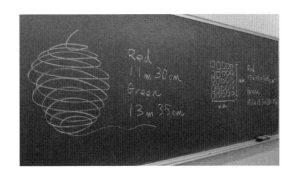

Designing Everything, Down to the Observational Process

Next, the students measured the length of the cords. They ran out of the classroom and looked for more spacious places in the school where they could stretch them out. The longest one in this particular class measured 11.3 m. Though the length varied depending on the type and size of the apple, by substituting a single piece of cord for the apple, the students discovered that the apple was much longer than they had expected. It will be immediately obvious when you look at the pictures, but converting the observed length into a distance filled the students with a sense of surprise: "Wow, the apple's circumference was this long!" In other words, by three- dimensionally visualizing distance through the use of people, cords, and spaces, it was possible to make the apple's circumference life-sized. If we take a look back at the observations in this chapter, we realize the following things: 1) We considered the necessity to devise a flexible notion to fit the circumstances by measuring the circumference of an apple, and as a result, we learned how to be constantly conscious of the "act of making." 2) By subtracting some information, we became aware of things that we were not able to see before. 3) We discovered that a fusion of functional beauty and emotional beauty leads to a sense of satisfaction. 4) By undoing

the cord in one go, we became aware of the importance of transience, sorrow, and gallantry. 5) By replacing length with distance, we figured out how to give it a physical form and actually experience the length. How can we now convey the entire process in a beautiful and easy-to-understand way? This is the point at which the theme of "conveying" enters the design. Now, we have to supplement our information with a sense of beauty. I want to make this a workshop that is completely filled with beautiful learning, from observation to expression. That is the concept I devised as the design for this course. In other words, I designed a way of learning that I want to share every aspect of with you. This is the key to conveying quality in communication.

03 | Apple: Observation—Area

I Never Thought of Doing It Like That Before!

I asked my students to devise a method of measuring the surface area of an apple. Despite my use of the term "surface area," I was not asking for precise dimensions. I said I wanted them to come up with a flexible concept like the answer to a riddle. One student suddenly suggested that we could peel the apple and then measure it. His idea was to cut the peel into small pieces, arrange them in a rectangle, and determine the area. It was a simple, clear idea. Next, I asked them how we could measure a plaster bust, the kind of thing used in a drawing class. Peeling was not an option in this case. They seemed deeply perplexed. I suggested that we could apply clay to the bust and then peel it off. If there was not a peel, you could make one. Then, as with the apple, you could divide the clay into small pieces, arrange it, and then measure it. Calculating precise dimensions is important, but I wanted them to realize that the ability to apply a certain skill would allow them to deal with a variety of conditions and circumstances in a flexible way. Having the vision to create a flexible concept is a valuable skill in design. The use of specialized machinery requires training, time, and money. The idea is to devise something out of easily obtainable, every-day objects, and trigger a realization like, "I never thought of doing it like that before!" We discover new values in attractive things. The act of peeling an apple flows naturally into the act of eating. This is something we have seen any number of times since childhood. It is easy to grasp when you imagine a three-dimensional object as a plane. But this application does

not work when it comes to a plaster bust. There was a time when design was called "applied art." In design, it is essential that the application conform to the actual circumstances. That means we must have the ability to properly understand, analyze, and express.

The goal of this workshop is to help you sense things through the experience of practical learning not impractical theory. Practical learning is the study of things that are useful in real life. Yukichi Fukuzawa, the founding father of Keio University, advocated and attached great importance to practical learning: "A spirit of independence in the

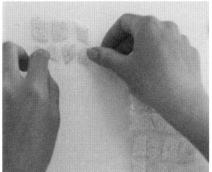

realm of the intangible is preferable to mathematics (theories and proofs) in the realm of the tangible." Along with medicine, law, and economics, design is a practical discipline. If we adapted Fukuzawa's words to fit the study of design, we might say, "A sense of beauty in the realm of the intangible is preferable to design (concepts and expressions) in the realm of the tangible."

This workshop should be a place of realization where you sense something physically and a place of learning where you acquire skills that can be applied to daily life.

The Ability to Read, Edit, and Redraw a Map

I see the peel that we spread out to measure the surface area of an apple as a map filled with an abundance of information. Information such as color, pattern, texture, and luster are coordinates that indicate "deliciousness." Just as some doctors see people's skin as a manifestation of their inner organs, information related to the substance of an apple appears on its peel. Using a superb method of conveying information about a generally complex distribution of land in two dimensions, a map is a reduced expression of part or all of the earth. Maps, said to date to a time when human culture still lacked things like the written word, are an indispensable part of our activities and daily life.

If we reexamine the apple as a map, it might be possible to arrive at some kind of realization. For example, by juxtaposing meteorological data with a production and distribution chart for apples, which are suited to cold regions, we begin to understand the problem of global warming. This sends out a warning about our way of living in regard to the environment, economy, and energy. A map also functions as a ruler for interpreting complex social conditions. We must be able to read, edit, and redraw maps.

Understand, observe, imagine, analyze, revise, and finally, visualize. The realizations contained in each of these processes give rise to a concept. Reading a map requires the ability to understand and observe. And to edit a map, we must be able to imagine, and analyze and restructure information. Having the ability to redraw the map with new values is also desirable. A small apple map seen as a wider world acts as a mirror of many things, even human activities.

Erasing the Name

I was surprised to see how beautiful the apple peels looked on the students' desks. I had the sense that by converting a three-dimensional object into a plane, the concept of an apple as I knew it had receded into the distance. But there was also something familiar about it. The peels had a beauty that reminded me of rose petals. When I looked around for

Rosaceae,
genus *Malus*,
tall deciduous tree

more information, I found this: "Rosaceae, genus *Malus*, tall deciduous tree." So apples really were part of the rose family. Does it not sometimes seem as if your imagination is so dominated by a concept that you can barely move? In that case, try erasing the name. By erasing something's name, you are peeling off its label and allowing its pure essence to emerge. This is the very basis of observation: Get rid of imprinted information and your own prejudices, and confront the subject. This helps expand the imagination. Look at things with your own eyes, touch them with your own hands, and explain your feelings in your own words. Expressions emerge from this kind of ordinary thing. Then, there is a need for criticism. In art, literature, and culture, criticism refers to the discussion of quality in regard to the concept and craftsmanship of a given work. This allows us to see things in a wider scope and discover a range of values. It is also sometimes necessary for design to be equipped with a critical spirit. A direct translation of the name "Muji" or "Muji-rushi Ryohin" a Japanese company that provides new values for living, would be "quality products without a brand [or name]." If we change our perspective slightly, we might also say that the company maintains a critical attitude toward "things that have a name but are lacking in quality." It is reasonable to think that every type of expression is supported by a certain critical attitude. At the same time, we might also say that the link I noticed between the beauty of rose petals and apple peels was a latent, unchanging connection that exists deep within these things. I did not know if there was a genetic link between roses and apples, but I intuitively discovered a relationship between their beautiful petals and peels. This relationship remains long after the names disappear and the ideas vanish. This leads to an awareness that enables us to discover a concept. Design is produced by two things: the ability to criticize and the ability to connect.

Attaching a Name

As one proverb would have it, "Names and natures do often agree." This suggests that the name of a person or thing often indicates its substance. What does naming something actually mean? It is a way of clearly distinguishing between two entities. To clarify the reason for something's existence, we must firmly comprehend the principles on which it is founded. A principle is the fundamental notion of how a certain thing should be, and by clearly determining your principles, you can achieve a sense of consistency in regard to your own words and deeds. That is, searching for a single word to express a principle is the act of attaching a name to something. Thus, a name gives voice to a principle.

On the other hand, it is best to construct a principle while making the most of the potential and vision of a given subject before the principle has been determined and prior to the emergence of the subject or after the subject has emerged but while it wanders in a chaotic state without any clear principle. But, because for the most part a sense of consistency in principle and activity overlaps with experience and history even in the case of a person or company that functions on the basis of clear principles, there is a need to enhance your principles and bring your activities closer in line with your principles. So, names and natures do often agree.

Let's imagine, for example, that the concept of the apple has vanished and that there are four boxes covered with peels. Let's give each one a name. We might write words like "apple," "rose," and "red" on each of the boxes. Each word brings out the potential contained in an apple through the use of a name that predates the disappearance of the concept, the name of a variety of apple, and the name of a color. Instead of giving the last box a name, we will leave it blank. Looking at the three names, we might imagine that "apple" is a drink, "rose" a fragrance, and "red" the color of something. Next, we search for the true character of the unnamed thing and try our best to stir our imaginations but no image is forthcoming. Names point us in a certain direction.

Brands attempt to make a qualitative difference between two products or services and to evoke a principle or activity on the basis of a name. Simply put, the act of branding means to create a bond with people and society. If we transposed branding into human terms, we could divide it into three broad categories: creating an emotion (or mental identity), creating a face (or visual identity), and creating a body (or behavioral identity). To create an emotion, you must permeate the subject with a principle. To create a face, the principle must be intelligibly verbalized and visualized as a design. And to create a body, you must introduce a mechanism based on the principle and connect it to an activity that anyone can perform. It is necessary to have all of these things. Though it is also true for upgrading a product or service, you are essentially asking society to justify the meaning of your own existence through all of your activities based on a given principle. This leads to the establishment of a brand.

04 | Apple: Observation—Color

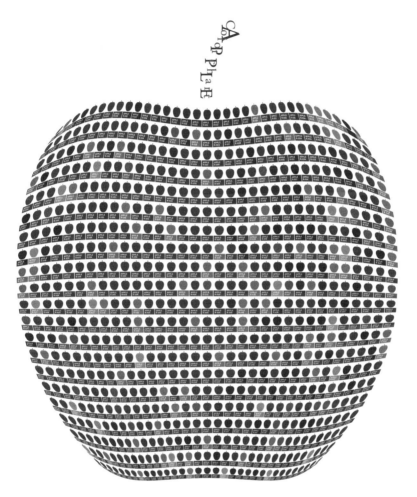

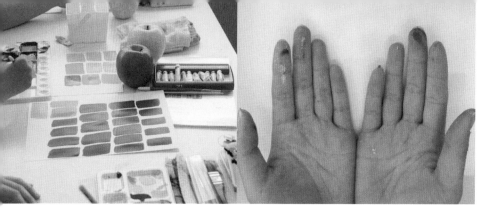

Colors Speak to Us

First, I asked the students to extract as many colors from an apple as they could. Then they narrowed them down to a hundred target colors. Next, they mixed some paint and matched the colors. Their fingertips were smeared with different colors, and through this series of actions, the colors assumed a physical form.

Observing colors does not mean merely looking at them. Colors have a texture, smell, rhythm, and taste. The quest for the colors concealed within the apple requires us to activate all five senses.

To become truly aware of color, we have to understand the principles of optics. Colors are reproduced through light, as I will discuss in more detail in a section called "Does a Rainbow Really Have Seven Colors?" In the meantime, let's talk about mixing colors. By mixing colors, we come to understand their structure. Not only do we have to know the difference between the three primary colors and the red-green-blue (RGB) color model, we have to physically experience colors by actually mixing them without relying on a color chart.

By working with paint, we come to understand the properties of colors, and how they can change depending on the combination of colors and materials. To get to know colors a little better, we can compare them

to people. Each color has a certain feeling, or more precisely, colors stimulate our emotions.

Coming into contact with the myriad colors concealed in an apple allows us to converse with them. Some colors are reticent, while others are garrulous. When we listen to colors, we find that like the various timbres of the instruments in an orchestra, each one speaks to us in a different way. Sometimes a color whispers seductively. Other times, like when red and blue are placed side by side, they glaringly command our attention. Neutral colors appear quiet at first, but they have an emotional side.

Try printing black on top of a color gradation. By approximating pitch black (the color created by layering black on the three primary colors), a rainbow arises out of the darkness. Actually, the rainbow was already present when the black was first printed on top of the color gradation, but it was too subtle for most people to immediately recognize. Adding the pitch black, however, brought out the color phase hidden within it.

Colors play tricks on our minds. The reason people have traditionally written characters and symbols in a uniform black was to avoid being tricked by them. It is not that colors lie; it is that our brains foster illusions. Understanding colors also offers us insight into the human mind.

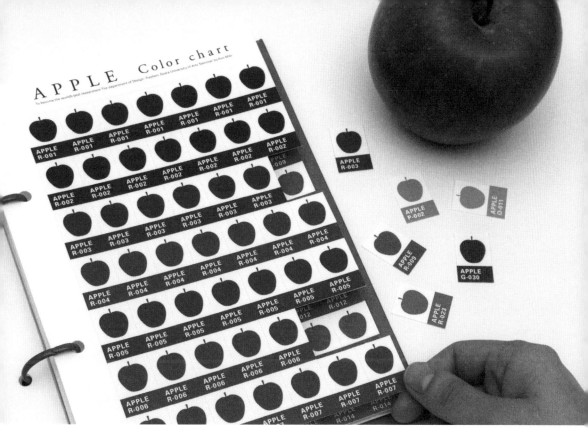

Freeing and Sharing Colors

Compared to the infinite variety of colors in nature, those in a commercial book of color samples are limited. You may not always find the color you want. The colors, the papers, and the typography we unthinkingly use day to day do not occur naturally. Someone had to design them. So if you cannot find the color you are looking for, why not design your own original book of samples?

The students used the various colors they found to make a book of apple colors. No two colors are alike in it, and no other sample book could contain such a rich variety of reds. There is a sweet red faintly tinged with yellow, a sour red subtly suffused with green, and an acerbic red with a generous dose of brown. Browsing through this book is like exchanging your eyes for your taste buds.

Of course, there is more to apples than just red. We arouse all of our senses to the legion of colors an apple contains, learn from the colors of nature, and attune ourselves to their richness and depth.

Colors can change depending on who is mixing them, just like flavors change depending on the dish and the chef. Take an apple and grate it into a dish, and soon it will start turning brown. This happens when the polyphenol contained in apples comes into contact with oxygen. Think of the smooth pale brown of apple sauce, a popular baby food. Then there is apple jam. Peel an apple, soak it in salt water, then simmer it with sugar, lemon, and cinnamon, and you will end up with yellow, translucent apple jam. To make red apple jam, soak the apple peel in salt water and add it to the simmering mix, then remove it once it is turned a pleasant shade of red.

The point here is not to share favorite jam recipes, but to point out that using the right procedures will produce enticing shades of red and yellow. Next, imagine a fresh-baked apple pie, its filling a deep golden yellow with a rich, tantalizing moistness you could not find in a fresh, uncooked apple. In cooking, colors change completely depending on the ingredients and how you prepare them. The same is true in printing—the same color will look utterly different when printed on a different kind of paper. Editing and combining colors entails exploring them from every possible angle.

So what is the best way for people to share color information with one another? As people found ways to answer this question, the commercialization of color arose. Commercialization means systematizing by color and material in accordance with purpose, usage, time constraints, and other relevant factors. Color sample books contain code numbers for each color that tell the precise percentage of base colors to mix, and the number alone can communicate a specific color to someone thousands of miles away. Colors, a subjective sensory experience, can be shared through sample books, and accurately reproduced anytime, anywhere. Colors are mass-produced and distributed as an industrial product, then recombined in packages for further distribution. Colors are liberated, flowing freely through our everyday lives, and becoming everyone's property.

Does a Rainbow Really Have Seven Colors?

Observing colors means observing light. In pitch darkness nothing, including an apple, has a color. To experience its color we need three elements: the apple itself, light, and our sense of sight. In more scientific terms, light is a type of electromagnetic wave, and when light at certain wavelengths passes through the retina, it stimulates the visual centers of the brain and registers as color.

Passing white light through a prism generates a rainbow-like beam called a spectrum. It just so happens that the man who discovered this and decreed that the rainbow has seven colors was Isaac Newton, famously said to have been inspired to formulate the law of universal gravitation by an apple falling from a tree. Renowned for his studies of the mechanics of nature, Newton also turned his attention to mathematics and optics.

You may have tried holding a prism up to the sunlight, but you certainly did not see a rainbow beam divided sharply into seven colors. The boundaries between colors are fuzzy, with smooth gradations from one to the next. Rather than the notes of a piano climbing the scale, colors are like the sliding notes of a trombone, one continuous progression.

As we can see in the gradual ripening of an apple, nature is full of such smooth transitions, like the four seasons slowly flowing into one another. The colors of the rainbow also gradually flow into one another, and Newton no doubt realized this. So why did he declare that there were seven colors? In Europe at the time, seven was considered a sacred number, and people sought it out in music and in natural phenomena. Some theorize

that Newton assigned the rainbow seven colors to match the seven intervals of the octave or the sacred seven of the Bible. Children in Japanese schools today are taught science based on the Newtonian tradition, and naturally grow up to see the rainbow as having seven colors. But ask people from other regions, other ethnic backgrounds, and other eras how many colors the rainbow has, and you might get a different answer.

In nature, there are an infinite number of colors. A culture of colors arises when people seek out the colors lurking between one color and the next. Examining the question of whether a rainbow really has seven colors can help train the eye. The eye here means the power of discernment, which combines insight, critical intellect, aesthetic appreciation, and other factors. The eye makes the designer. The objective of this chapter was to dismantle the preconception that "apples are red," and to draw attention to the richly varied natural palette that apples contain.

05 | Apple : Doodling

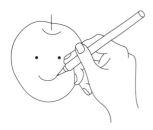

The Search for Hidden Meanings

After completing our observation of apples, the next step is to use apple peels to create doodles. This is a warm-up exercise to loosen up the imagination. The important thing is to relax and hum along as you are doing it.

With apples as a common starting point, people strike off in an amazing variety of directions. Some associate apple peels with throwing away garbage, and decide to depict animals or other ecology-related motifs. Others make the obvious connection of apples with eating, and create images of mouths or food. Others turn the random shapes of apple peels into an abstract design element, while still others broadly interpret apples as symbols of a happy lifestyle. Creating doodles may seem on the surface like an aimless endeavor, but this activity is different from merely doodling on a blank page. It is a method of seeking out the structures, forms, and colors in the apple, and of finding relationships to other things.

While performing this activity, people search for hidden meanings. With movements of their hands, they spark a dialogue with the subject matter and explore its potential. They find relationships, and sublimate narrow meanings to larger concepts. This process contains the fundamental elements of design, and even more importantly it fosters a love of learning. As the creator's heart skips lightly, his or her true personality

Speaking design

floats to the surface. Reading between the lines of charming doodles, we can sense the creator's playful character, and their drive to delight and entertain. The power of humor to facilitate communication is truly magical.

Speaking Design and Listening Design

Painting a picture is a way of initiating a dialogue with the subject. Design is a way of engaging in a dialogue with society. Of course, a dialogue means a repeated cycle of speaking and then listening to what the other person has to say and understanding what they think.

We do not need to keep the word "apple" in mind to carry out repeated observations and trigger verbal associations. In fact, we may draw closer to the truth without words. Just as unspoken words can find expression through one's manner of action, the internal condition of an apple, or something else can be deduced from its color, markings, and hardness. To observe someone or something, we must turn our ears to that person or thing, listening intently as we would when conducting an interview, and comprehending. This is where it all begins. Understanding means deepening trust. Making sense of what the subject has to say, and making clarification your top priority—within this process lie virtually all of the issues that design is intended to resolve. I refer to this as "listening design."

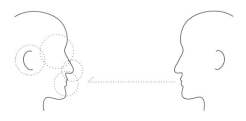

Listening design

And what of speaking? It means communicating one's ideas clearly to others. Dialogue is not a one-way street. Sometimes it takes detours and strays from the topic. Doodling with apples is one example. Some people make leaps so great that they seem to be completely unrelated to the subject, but these should not be rejected out of hand. They may communicate ideas at a higher frequency that is only audible to younger people. They may generate new values, form connections, and point the way to fresh ideas. Even when people make excessive leaps of thought and seem to be drifting too far from the shore, they sometimes have an anchor that is invisible to others. Dialogue is a laboratory for new discoveries, which are encounters with things or phenomena previously unknown to humanity, or at least to the person who finds them. When you discover something, you become enraptured with curiosity and want to communicate your discovery to other people. Giving visible form to these discoveries is what I call "speaking design." Engaging in a dialogue with apples, and searching.

Exhibiting and Voting on the Works

Once everyone has created apple doodles, it is time to line them all up on the desks for an exhibition. Each person is given three Post-Its, which they affix to the works they are especially fond of. Voting for one's own work is, naturally, forbidden. Each person explains what they think is great about the pieces they chose, making a kind of campaign speech for them. When presented with all the doodles, each person gets a clear sense of how their ideas and execution measure up, and pays attention to the criteria others are using to make judgments. Everyone's expression grows serious.

People whose doodles received votes step forward holding their works, while those who chose them discuss why they did. Some students may have more than one of their pieces selected. Under the gaze of the entire class, their embarrassed grins can be seen gradually shifting to confident ones. Meanwhile, those whose doodles were not selected seem to be steeling themselves for the next time around.

Exhibiting the works together, and voting on them, gives each person a sense of where their own creations stand. Hearing objective opinions from others helps people to really see their own works. They gain confidence, or a stronger drive to succeed. Or they may be devastated. Each student has the power to evaluate his or her own work without the instructor saying a word.

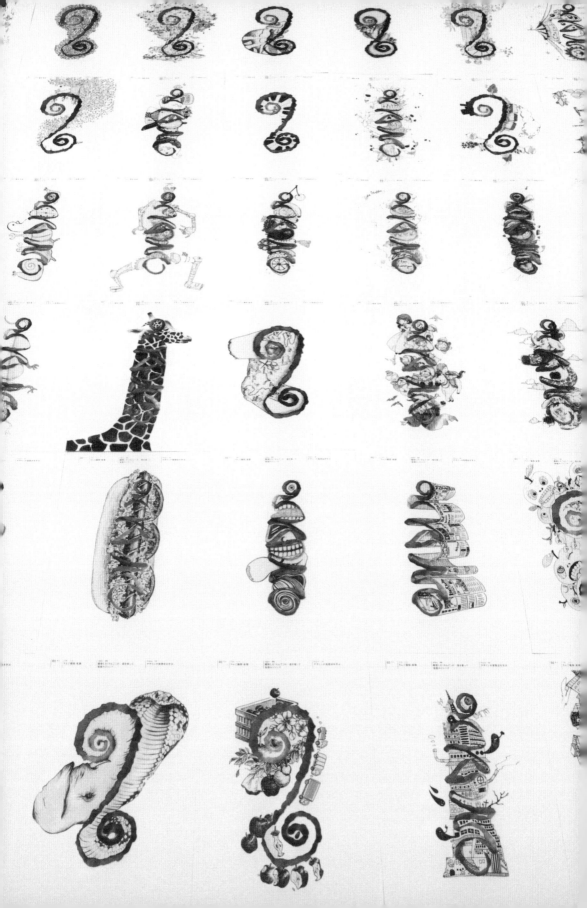

06 | Apple: Points

Think Big, Act Small

Toothpicks are small, thin pieces of wood with sharp tips, generally used for removing things trapped between the teeth, or for sticking in food items such as hors d'oeuvres. They are inexpensive and can be found in just about any Japanese household. They can also be used to create a pointillist painting of an apple. Of the basic elements that form a picture, namely points, lines and planes, this painting employs points alone, clustered together to simulate a plane.

Think of a cube of sugar. Assuming that the grains of sugar in the cube are points, then the sides of the cube are planes composed of points. Meanwhile, the edges where two sides meet are lines formed from a progression of points. Indeed, the entire three-dimensional object consists of points. Now, by exchanging the familiar paintbrush for a toothpick and painting with points alone, we shall attune ourselves to the dense information lurking in colors and areas of light and shadow.

We are taught that we should switch implements freely to suit the task at hand, and we take this ability for granted. Here, however, the rule is that we may only use a toothpick. By being forced to paint with nothing but small dots, we can hone our awareness of detail. The famous quote from German architect Ludwig Mies van der Rohe, "God is in the details," springs to mind. The intensity of colors and the fineness of textures strike us differently from when we are painting with brushes.

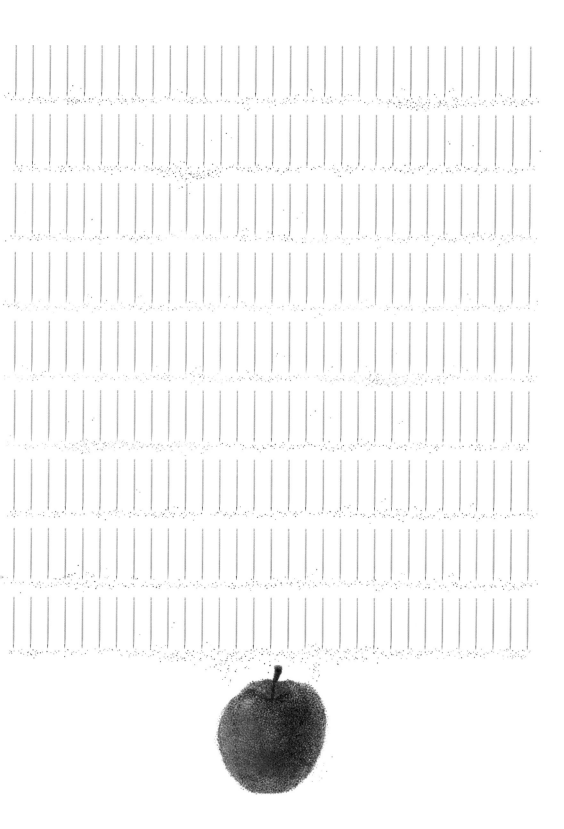

When we paint with brushes, they become extensions of our arms, but with toothpicks we are robbed of freedom of movement and experience mounting frustration. We are flummoxed by the difficulty of portraying an overall form as a collection of points. As in the proverb about not seeing the forest for the trees, being engrossed in minute details keeps us from seeing the big picture, and our flustered brains struggle to call forth their comprehensive powers of observation. Questions are asked and answered. The process strengthens the imaginative powers needed to put a collection of parts together into a whole. This is the "think big, act small" approach advocated by the ancient Chinese philosopher and Confucian scholar Xunzi: Look at things from an all-encompassing perspective, but then put things into practice one tiny step at a time. That is the concept behind this workshop. From parts to a whole, and then back again. Here, both the insect's compound eye and the bird's far-reaching vision are required.

Learning from Limitations

In the never-ending pursuit of a more convenient lifestyle, design often emphasizes functional value above all. However, as life grows more convenient, there are things that are lost or dulled. I notice that an increasing number of students are unable to peel an apple with a knife or to sharpen a pencil with a utility blade, and it has become necessary to provide students with peelers rather than knives. Some of them have never peeled an apple before in their lives.

Failing to carry out a task like peeling or sharpening can open our eyes to the preciousness of things, and the importance of making do with the tools at hand as we work toward a goal. With the progress of computer technology, designers' work environments have drastically changed. Today, anyone can make something that passes for typographic design simply by selecting a font and typing on a keyboard, but when I started out as a designer, people had to trace each letter onto tracing paper, adjust the

size of the text with a photographic enlarger, and then trace the letters again. Then they colored them in, and finally the lettering was completed. It was a time-consuming and labor-intensive process, but by repeating it many times we gained skill in drawing letters and our work grew more polished. If we traced sloppily, the final outcome was sure to be skewed, and redoing it from the start meant a sleepless night. That hammered a lesson into us that we learned with every bone in our bodies. This is not to say that limitations are desirable, but time-consuming, labor-intensive processes cause us to incorporate ideas and techniques physically so they come to be as natural as breathing. Imposing the limitation of painting points with a toothpick makes for a creative exercise that reignites our relationship with the physical.

Bringing a Still Life to Life

Watching pointillist paintings in progress, as they start out faint and grow progressively darker in color, is like watching a time-lapse video of an apple ripening. Dots of color sandwiched among other colors gradually create a sense of depth. This is what makes this process of generating an apple different from the act of tracing its outlines. Unlike a still life, these pictures are not still but dynamic, seeming to depict the passage of time.

If a fully ripe apple sat before us, we could observe its color change from red to reddish brown, then to rust brown and finally to a red-tinged black. Sitting down to paint a pointillist apple after this experience, we would probably depict an overripe apple well along on the path from life to death. Naturally, this would require some degree of expressive technique, but it would be no mere still life. It would literally seem to come to life. Observing the changes in shape and color as life ebbs away and death sets in, noticing the gradual changes of the natural world, learning the laws of nature—design, too, lies within this realm of activity.

CMY Pointillism

During the class on observing the color of apples, I explained that the three primary colors were cyan, magenta, and yellow (often abbreviated CMY), and that in printing black (K) is added, and an aggregation of tiny halftone dots in these four colors form images. Later, when we were about to do pointillist paintings, a student asked if they were required to use the colors they had assembled in their apple color sample books. I had planned the exercise so that students would become acquainted with the cornucopia of colors concealed within the apple, then use these myriad colors to depict apples, and discover something like an organic growth process in which layers of color create a richly expressive apple. When I asked the student what she meant, she replied that she would like to try using only the three

colors CMY, apparently noting the similarity between the toothpick dots of a pointillist picture and the halftone dots of printing.

I thought this was a truly brilliant idea, just the kind of stroke of inspiration this course was intended to trigger. I spoke about it to the rest of the class, and specially allowed just the one student to paint the apple using only CMY in the manner of halftone printing. I imagine that to produce mixed colors by adjusting the number of dots of each primary color was quite a difficult task, requiring the imagination to be running full throttle. However, if you add black into the mix you have the mechanism of printing right there, and this was a way of absorbing this mechanism physically. I am thinking of incorporating the student's idea into the next course.

I have gained new ideas like this one from students so many times that it might seem as if I planned the workshop for that very purpose. Just because you carry out a program again and again does not mean you have to get stuck in a rut of simple repetition. Instructors get stuck in ruts because they cease to notice the flashes of inspiration provided by students' creations and suggestions. To design a course of study requires being open to new ideas, and having the flexibility to adjust the program to the needs of each individual.

07 | Apple : Line

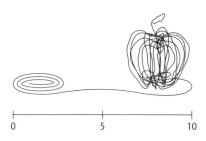

0   5   10

Thinking with the Hands

In the chapter "Apple: Observation—Length," we measured the circumference of an apple. Let us now prepare some wire with a length equivalent to this circumference, and create an apple object. The pre-defined length imposes restrictions on design while at the same time offering flexibility within these restrictions. You might say that the point of this project is to examine the processes people undertake in creating something out of this limited material.

Some make preparatory sketches, others gaze at the wires and plot out an idea, while others simply take it in their hands and let their intuition guide them. Everyone is different, but in the end it is the hands that do the work. The fingertips have been called the antennae of the brain, and this makes sense because they contain concentrated bundles of nerves that lead directly to the brain. When humans began walking upright, their hands were freed to explore, and the resulting stimuli drove the development of higher brain functions. The concentration of nerves in the fingertips animates the brain and activates the imagination.

The body springs forward first, and logic plods along afterward. As if they were shaping clay, the students move their bodies and let their imaginations run free, guiding the material in their hands toward the shape they have described in their heads. To turn an image in the mind into

a three-dimensional shape naturally requires thinking and working in three dimensions—width, depth, and height: in short, spatial reasoning capacity. This is the capacity to grasp how a space is occupied and the various relationships within it instantaneously, and to react to it accurately. It is the same skill we use to extrapolate three-dimensional terrain features from a map or a set of contour lines. Athletes employ spatial reasoning when they catch a ball that comes toward them or aim a ball toward a particular spot. Animals use it to protect themselves from enemies and survive.

An important element of this skill set is intuition, a loose term encompassing powers of observation, sensitivity, and innate aptitude. Observing the students with this in mind, it is easy to spot hands guided by intuition. The fingers appear to be feeling space instinctively, reacting with heightened sensitivity, and indeed thinking for themselves. In reality, of course, the brain is controlling them with the help of various sensory organs of touch and sight. Sometimes the hands produce unexpected shapes seemingly of their own accord, and at these times the fingertips are delighted at the random form and become deeply engrossed in it. The hands have awareness, so if the brain is stuck on a concept it is a good idea to leave it up to the hands. This does not mean a merely hit-or-miss approach. It means that the hands think while they are moving, just like people tend to think while they are running. Perhaps this is the very essence of visual design.

An Aerial Apple

Watching students produce apples using wire, one sees the same range of movements a conductor's baton makes in front of an orchestra—sweeping movements that envelop the air, delicate movements that make the air quiver, occasionally bold movements that seem to splatter space. The conductor communicates his interpretation of a piece of music and the accompanying expressive points to the musicians, who absorb his intent, and the piece of music takes form. The conductor's baton is a tool that gives visual expression to musical processes, and he uses it to depict music in space the way a painter uses a brush to paint a picture on canvas. The students' wire is analogous to the baton, as they use it to depict a spatial entity—the apple—within space. This space within a space, like a soap bubble floating in the air, seems to be both "here" and "there," moving on a different temporal axis.

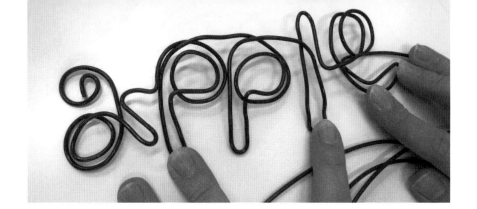

Creating ideas and works of design means presenting new values and new forms within the spatial continuum of our daily lives. To this endeavor each designer brings his or her own unique character, manifested as originality, or directness, or humor. Like the world inside a soap bubble, what the students create is both "here," in this world, and "there," drifting in its own self-contained universe, searching for something. The process of searching gives rise to original, sometimes antithetical ideas, and in the end arrives at its object—a mysterious something that, like air, is invisible to the eye but absolutely necessary for life. The process also gives rise to ideas of coexistence and empathy. Another apple has appeared alongside the familiar physical apples that grow on trees. Let us call it an aerial apple.

Writhing Perseverance

The three-dimensional wire apples are gradually taking shape. Some people have started at the core and built outwards to create a skeletal apple. Others have stitched together a surface as if doing embroidery. One person's hands move rapidly as if they were doing a rough sketch of a live model. Another has created a design incorporating the word "apple." Still another has simply wrapped the wire around and around, as if they encountered a creative block along the way. The variety of apples is truly impressive.

What they all have in common is that they differ radically from the real apples measured in the "Apple: Observation—Length" chapter. Placed side by side, they resemble myriad varieties of apple lined up in the supermarket. Some look more like pumpkin squashes or oranges, but each one is certainly unique. The individuality of each creator peeks through, making it possible to enjoy both the technical prowess of accurate depictions and the idiosyncrasy of offbeat ones. The class has truly breathed life into their apples, which look ready to speak.

Behind them all lie the solitary struggles of each creator. Some struggle with the length of wire itself, while others are perturbed by the other creations taking shape around them, and still others are anxious about running out of time. All seem to be posing themselves repeated questions and coming up with answers. Creating a work of art is always an ongoing struggle. It is solitary, lonely, and sometimes brings one to the verge of tears. Originality shines forth as we seek to overcome this adversity, floundering, and writhing. In the midst of this shines a ray of light. "Writhing perseverance" is, as it seems to me, at the root of all creative endeavors.

08 | Apple: Word-association Game

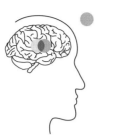
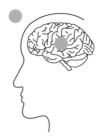

Brain-borrowing

Each person in a group tries individually to think of a hundred words associated with apples. Red, sweet, Snow White, Steve Jobs... The words come to mind one after another, but for some people they start to peter out after just thirty words. For most people, fifty or so is the limit. The way to reach a hundred is to call a time-out. Set aside a designated length of time for the group to borrow one another's brains by going over the words they have come up with thus far, and then start word-associating again.

"Brain-borrowing" may be an unfamiliar phrase, but it is one I often use to describe the process of coming into contact with other people's ideas to broaden the scope of one's own. In Japanese, the phrase is *shakuno*, which recalls *shakkei*, the technique of "borrowing scenery" that is used in many Japanese and Chinese gardens. This means interpreting the natural scenery surrounding a garden as a part of the garden itself. The practice of incorporating the scenic backdrop into the garden's overall design was introduced to Japan during the Heian Period (794–1185), and was most prevalent from the Edo Period (1603–1868) through the pre-World War II era.

Apply this idea of uniting foreground and background to society, and you see the potential for coexistence, cooperation, and growth. *Shakuno*

suggests people seeing things in new ways and unearthing new treasures by incorporating one another's ideas. When I declare that it is brain-borrowing time and the workshop participants share the word-associations they have made so far, expressions grow serious and each person begins to confront their own ideas head-on. Mental blocks fall, and thought processes start to move freely again like fish returned to water. When the word-association game recommences, rigidified brains have been limbered up and it does not take long for each person to reach their hundred words.

The next step is to categorize and color-code the words everyone has come up with. Red and green are colors, sweet and sour are tastes, Snow White and William Tell are characters in stories, Steve Jobs and Sir Isaac Newton are people. Words are assigned a category and categories are assigned a color. This process focuses the mind on content and, as you might imagine, adds further impetus to the word-association game. Once the process has been codified in this way, it becomes like a clear-cut diagram that inspires each participant, fueling his or her unique approach to the apple as a concept.

This workshop is divided into two sessions, with an entirely new crop of students in the second session. Be that as it may, some participants have clearly come prepared for this activity and have already got their apple-related words mentally sorted into categories before the activity

begins. However, this can cause them to get stuck within the framework they have constructed and make them run out of steam early. The way to approach this game is, first of all, to pull out all the stops and think of any and every apple-related word you can. Some words may appear to be far removed from the source, but they are all connected in the stream of consciousness, and letting things flow freely is the best way to uncover new ideas. Starting out by organizing into categories is putting the cart before the horse, and will cause the thought process to ossify. Things ought to start out disorganized, and then be further scattered by the brain-borrowing activity, so that everyone encounters ideas they never would have thought of on their own. Then it will be time for each person to sort and edit these ideas. The product of this word-association game will serve as the foundation for the remainder of the workshop.

Apple Correlation Charts

The apple word-association game has awakened the participants to the apple's wealth of content and the importance of focusing on content as opposed to form alone. Having brainstormed lists of words individually, the group now works together to create apple correlation charts, incorporating the technique of Mind Mapping. Advocated by British author and educator Tony Buzan, Mind Mapping is a thought and brainstorming technique that entails graphic expression of thought patterns. You begin by writing or drawing the main subject in the center of a sheet of paper, then write related keywords or draw pictures around it,

and repeat the process with each one of these to create a diagram of radiating, branching, color-coded lines. This renders the mind's internal processes visible.

Based on this concept, the students work together in groups to create their own apple correlation charts. They append pictures to words and fuel their creativity using brain-borrowing within each group. It is not necessary to adhere to the Mind Mapping technique. The point of this process is to give direct and compact expression to massive quantities of data, and to improve comprehension, memory, inventiveness, and problem-solving ability. Each group is supposed to come to a consensus on their own style of diagram, using the Mind Mapping concept as a guide. When the contents of the group's discussion are graphically expressed,

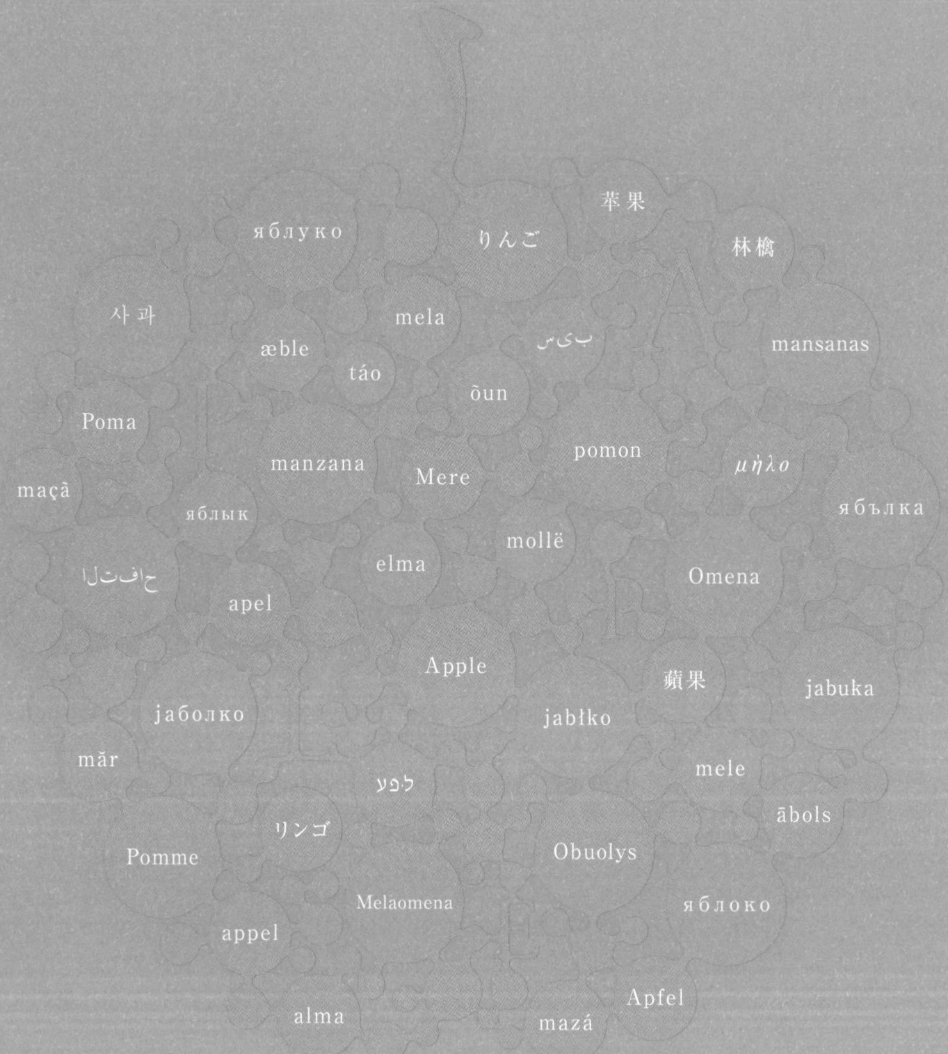

苹果

りんご

林檎

яблуко

с사과

mela

سیب

mansanas

æble

táo

ōun

Poma

manzana

pomon

μῆλο

maçã

Mere

яблык

ябълка

التفاح

mollë

Omena

elma

apel

Apple

蘋果

jabuka

jаболко

jabłko

măr

mele

תפוח

ābols

リンゴ

Obuolys

Pomme

яблоко

Melaomena

appel

Apfel

alma

mazá

the mental processes and mutual brain-borrowing of the group become visible as well, and the participants watch ideas and values different from their own gain concrete form. Words arising through association connect with key words in other categories, and people gain insight into the truly complex, three-dimensional process unfolding inside the brain.

A key question is how to put thought patterns, which spread and proliferate like ivy, into manageable form. Each team has its own solution: some teams put their complex webs of mental connections into the shape of an apple, others express the chaos of random thought-encounters as a labyrinth, while still others use a large number of pictures to make their chart instantly and intuitively graspable. These diagrams come to look like nothing so much as microcosms of the universe, world or society. Condensing everything down to this size is an important act. When information is too vast to be taken in at a glance, we are plunged into chaos. A map works because it shows you the entire terrain at once, but is small enough to fold up and put in your pocket. If everything contained in your brain were drawn on paper at actual size, you would have an extremely large sheet of paper. To see the big picture, you need a picture small enough to fit in your field of vision. Seeing and understanding the way things connect is the key to remembering, inventing, and solving problems. In this activity, team members establish mutual understanding and solidify their themes and intentions, and this understanding forms the basis for all the further connections they will make.

09 | Apple: Party

Communication, Hospitality, and Art

The entire class is invited to an apple party off campus at my design studio, Ken Miki & Associates. Each student brings his or her own elaboration of the apple motif to the party, from costumes to accessories. Somehow the general excitement level seems a bit higher than it is during classes. Playfulness and inspiration are in the air, and everyone has applied their design sensibilities to the task of entertaining themselves and putting smiles on each other's faces.

My staff at the studio has been busy cooking up food and creating utensils with an apple theme. The object is to demonstrate the true meaning of hospitality to the students. At the same time, I want the staff to get a sense of how their creations affect the taste buds and other sensory organs by observing the students' reactions firsthand. A close-up look at someone's thrilled response to hospitality is a picture of customer satisfaction and appreciation that could never be gained through facts and figures.

This apple party is not mere fun and games. It is an activity that takes cues from the sophisticated variations and substitutions, the spirit of hospitality and communication of the tea ceremony. Many people think of the tea ceremony as merely a set of ritualized procedures for preparing tea and serving it to guests, and another set of procedures for being served tea, but there is more to it than that. It is a composite art

form encompassing cuisine, sweets, hanging scrolls, flower arrangement, utensils, and other elements of hospitality, combined and harmonized in endless variations to suit the season, the time of day, the motif or the guests. The guests, in turn, absorb, and derive pleasure from the thoughtfulness of the host.

In a sense, all aspects of the hosts' and guests' communication and demeanor are an extension of the tea ceremony. Broadly defined, the tea ceremony is an art form with all manner of profound connections to design and lifestyle. The Japanese word for tea is *cha*, and we can turn this into an acronym: "C" for communication, "H" for hospitality, and "A" for art. This is the concept behind the apple party. The apple theme unites everyone in an environment that entertains, delights, amuses, and instructs.

Apples and Me

On the first day of the workshop, all of the participants introduced themselves by way of a performance with two elements: apples and themselves. Each student struck whatever poses he or she liked. These were captured on video, and played back at the apple party as eight-frame, stop-motion films. Everybody crowded around to watch the footage of their own performances, from a time when they were novices who had just met one another. One performer shyly offers an apple to the audience, another head-butts it, and still another juggles apples, each person acting on flashes of inspiration. When the stop-motion documents of these performances are shown back to back on a single screen, it is an opportunity for the students to study one another.

It is a study of human behavior, with the apple as a focal point, that reminds one of Modernology—a term, coined by Wajiro Kon in 1927, meaning to study and analyze social phenomena by observing customs

and conditions at designated times and places in a contemporary city. Modernology falls into the broader academic field of ethnology, and aims to do for the contemporary world what archaeology does for the ancient one. This discipline later inspired new developments in the study of lifestyles and customs and the observation of street life.

Each individual's personal background shapes his or her performance with apples, or substitutions of apples and other objects. The "apples and me" performance is a one-time-only, no-second-takes affair, showing the person as he or she is with no room for flubbing or bashfulness. Whatever is concealed inside the performer seems to leak out. Everyone comes to understand one another better.

In this way, people bond at my design studio and Team Miki gains new members. On the question of learning how to learn, it seems obvious that an environment where people enjoy themselves, and support, compete with, and admire one another, is an environment conducive to intellectual curiosity. Almost instantly, along with the desire to know comes the gumption to decide something, do it, and stick to it. My hope is that being part of the tight-knit community of Team Miki will foster a love of learning. After the apple party, it is interesting to note how students' levels of motivation change in the classroom. Close encounters with one another spark a flame that continues to burn long afterward.

10 | Apple: One Line

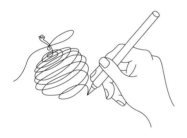

Connecting, Expanding, Discovering

Using the words the students assembled in the apple word-association game as hints, I asked them to draw pictures with a single line next. On either side of five small, 150 × 100 mm cards, the words "in" and "out," indicating the beginning and end of the line, were printed. Between these, they made pictures consisting of a single uninterrupted line. Retracing the line was not allowed, but crossing it was okay. With these rules as a foundation, they had to draw an apple. On the remaining four cards, they drew something inspired by the other words they had come up with in the word-association game.

Together, the five cards were a set of apples made up of one line. Each of them built up a story and developed an idea. For example, one student went from apple to Snow White to witch to a falling apple to the Beatles, and another went from apple to a girl with red cheeks like an apple to a gorilla with an apple to New York to Steve Jobs. They came up with their own stories as they made the pictures. And the pictures were all part of a linked sequence. Because the beginning and end of the line were always the same, even if you changed the order of the pictures, they would still connect. This was not only true for each person's pictures, but for everyone's cards.

Like a picture book for mental training, each viewer could freely create his or her own story. For instance, by merely connecting everyone's apple pictures, you could make a story out of a single line. Or by combining the pictures in different ways, you could create several different stories.

By connecting, expanding, and discovering, the single line that each student had drawn rapidly expanded. By restructuring this idea for the web, and developing it into a system that allowed everyone to contribute, you could connect the entire world. Before you knew it, the single line of one apple could expand into a whole forest of apples. The apple landscape, constantly altered by someone or other, would eventually provide an encounter with a magnificent story.

Simplification Accentuates Structure

By making a rule that the students could only draw a picture with a single line, they quickly anticipated that an object with a complex shape would grow even more complex through the meandering quality of the line. This led them to try and express the formal characteristics and structure of the object in a more lucid manner. This was because they were searching

for a sense of originality in a simple form just as they had when they made the pictograms. Also, because the small cards had a set size, it prevented them from trying to incorporate an excess of information.

When I first started studying design, I remember being taught that designing a poster was like designing a stamp. To come up with a rough sketch that fits inside a small stamp, you are forced to organize what you want to convey in a simple way, and in doing this, your message becomes clear. And a poster that looks big at arm's length actually looks like a stamp in the wider context of the city. In addition, by using the words that the students had come up within the word-association game as subject matter, everything that they drew created a story that was related to apples.

You sometimes meet someone who finds it hard to convey their message in conversation. That is because the content of their speaking is undecided. It is the same with a picture. That is why it is important to realize that the more complex the information is, the greater need there is to briefly summarize the content and main points, and accentuate it with a simplified structure. This results in a picture that is packed with information and conveyed in a speedy way.

While enjoying an activity that they probably did as children, they expressed a unique sense of individuality in each picture. For example, the

students devised a variety of ways to deftly express the thickness of an object by making the line loop back and forth, and imbued the picture with linear texture and pattern. This helped them realize that a certain amount of "inconvenience" can enrich a concept. Losing track of time as they pleasantly and excitedly drew, the students finished the set of five cards in no time at all. It was like communicating through pictographs. A single-line picture is another way of approaching the question, "What is illustration?"

Design, Environment, and Psychology

The students then made posters based on the stories they had developed with the single-line pictures. While some used ideas from the cards in their original form, and others made designs inspired by new concepts, all of them

puzzled at how to adapt the small cards to a format that was almost five times bigger (728 × 515 mm). I told them the same thing that I had learned as a student—design a poster as if it were a stamp. I also told them that there is a difference between designing the cover of a book and its text. I wanted them to design a cover, but I told them that by giving preference to the narrative of the single line, they would end up with a poster that had a strongly edited quality. But by realizing that the priority was on information, the poster would gradually become stronger.

The students were not allowed to use computers in any of the activities we did in the class. They had to make everything by hand. By approaching and distancing themselves from objects through the differences in each medium (small cards and big posters), they began to develop a physical sense of what design was. And they also learned to judge the actual size. This was intended to help them understand that making judgments based on a small computer screen can sometimes lead to major errors. Conceiving of a sign plan based on empty desktop speculation may lead to a total lack of function in the actual environment. After examining every aspect of an environment, from the shape, color, size, material, objective, situation, and medium to people's movements and visual illusions, we incorporate a design in our bodies. A functional design emerges out of three things: design, environment, and psychology.

11 | Apple: Onomatopoeia

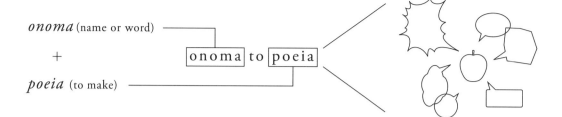

onoma (name or word)

\+

poeia (to make)

onoma to poeia

Wordless Words

The English word "onomatopoeia," derived from the Greek *onoma* (name or word) and *poeia* (to make), generally refers to words that express sounds in the world around us. Some words we think of as onomatopoeia do not express sounds but rather sensory perceptions or states of being. Onomatopoetic words in the narrow sense are transliterations of noises made by living or non-living things, such as the *whoosh* of air, the *splash* of water, and the *bow-wow* of a dog barking. In Japanese, dogs say *wan-wan*: just one example of how things sound different, or are perceived differently, depending on the country, culture or individual.

Onomatopoetic words that express physical conditions, behavior or emotive states (known variously as sound-symbolic words, mimetic words or ideophones) are extremely common in Japanese—examples include *kera-kera* (a belly laugh), *muka-muka* (the feeling of anger), *noshi-noshi* (the movements of a large man), and *yobo-yobo* (feebleness from old age). Incidentally, I once gave a lecture in South Korea through an interpreter. Afterward, I was surprised to have an attendee tell me the talk had been entertaining, "like a cartoon." When lecturing, I had spoken in short blocks and then paused while they were translated into Korean, and with all this stopping and starting I had been unable to get into a groove. Struggling to get my point across somehow, I had apparently fallen back on using large amounts of onomatopoeia, something like "When you

'squish' the concept into something more compact, it adds more 'oomph' to your message. Give it a light touch and deliver it with a 'zing.' People will respond with 'oohs' and 'aahs'!" The audience, who did not understand Japanese, heard this onomatopoeia peppering my speech before they grasped the meaning through the interpreter, and it made a strong impression on them.

Onomatopoeia is not the language of the rational, but of the corporeal, the emotional, and the spatial, allowing people to grasp a situation or scene intuitively. Like sound effects in movies, it provides people with vicarious experiences. There is onomatopoeia for psychological states as well. In kabuki, which has employed sounds for dramatic effect since the Edo Period (1603–1868), a supernatural frisson is expressed with a disquieting drum roll when ghostly characters take the stage. Onomatopoeia is a mode of sensory communication that conveys what does not fit into the logical structures of ordinary language. Comics and cartoons in particular are a treasure trove of onomatopoeia. Japan's manga and anime are global leaders in this field, and most people in Japan grew up immersed in written onomatopoeia, gaining an instinctive feel for the infusion of lettering with emotive content.

In my class, the next activity is to select onomatopoeia inspired by the apple, and design emotive bits of text like those seen in comics and cartoons. Students brainstorm sounds related to the apple—the *crunch* of

someone biting into an apple, the *thunk* of one falling from a tree, or the *shlurr-shlurr-shlurr* of one being peeled—and create typography for them. They are asked to bring comic books to class as references, and to start by looking through them and noting the correlations between onomatopoeia and typography. Next, they cut onomatopoetic text out of the manga and arrange it on sheets of paper. Isolated and decontextualized, the violence, lyricism, humor or misery of the typography is thrown into sharp relief. The wordless words manage to evoke a mental landscape despite the lack of inherent meaning or accompanying illustrations. Some of the students get so engrossed in the world of manga that they forget the original purpose of the exercise.

As a rule, people setting out to learn typography begin with its fundamental building blocks, the skeletal structures underlying lettering. Here, however, as a basic exercise for these budding young designers, we focus strictly on the physicality and emotional expressiveness that lettering can take on through typographic style.

Learning by Imitation

By making copies after other artists, replicating both the style and the content of specific works, we come to grasp their intent and gain command of their techniques. Here, the students begin by examining

the onomatopoeia in manga and noticing its sheer expressive range. They then write their own apple-related onomatopoeia in styles copied from manga, but despite this, the works they produce qualify as new material. Of course, this is not to deny the importance of originality. However, when students appropriate onomatopoeia but change the written characters to express different sounds, the resulting gap between form and content produces cognitive dissonance. As they struggle to adapt to the change in content and resolve this dissonance, their works gain distance from the source material, and the students gain ownership over them. An important aspect of copying is that of recognizing what you admire, and what direction you want to go. As you move in that direction, you get a closer look at and a more thorough understanding of the object of your admiration.

Seen from another angle, admiration feeds the desire to learn. We copy what we admire. I like to think that this helps us understand the intentions of those we admire, and gain some mastery of technique. When I was considering how best to convey the magic of typography to fledgling designers, it struck me that the onomatopoeia in manga, a medium in which many have been steeped since childhood, would easily pique their interest. However, I must admit I was uncertain about whether they could make written characters into full-fledged works of design. This led me to the idea of learning by imitation. I had some opportunities between classes to discuss the subject of copying with students, but once the workshop actually got underway I was surprised at how easily they took to it. After leafing through the classroom materials, many of them got started on rough sketches right away.

Japanese children are extremely adept at drawing comics, perhaps more so than kids anywhere else in the world. Many practically eat, sleep, and breathe manga, and on reaching adulthood have already internalized the onomatopoeia found in their pages. The stage is set for the creation of unique, diverse, inspired, and expressive onomatopoeia.

Design Resides in Relationships Between Subject and Object

We made posters depicting apples alongside the onomatopoetic typography that the students had created. Then further sound effects were added. Written characters already brimming with emotion become even more expressive. Onomatopoeia wriggles to life, seeming to move like a snippet of an animated film. One is reminded once again of how effectively lettering can convey gestures, emotions, and circumstances. Onomatopoetic typography, infused with feeling, can signify sizzle on a product's packaging, or manifest the mental state of a character in a novel. The possibilities are endless. Of course the written characters must be legible as text, but with the added element of affect, they take on dynamic personalities of their own. Onomatopoetic expressiveness

pervades the language of emotions toward people and things—gladness, sadness, anger, resignation, surprise, loathing, fear. At the same time, typefaces used in running text should never be loaded with emotion. Typeface design must prioritize legibility and aesthetic appeal.

Design resides in relationships between subject and object. The subjective is emotion-laden individual thought, while the objective is data-driven, generally accepted thought. At the same time, the subject is the person performing actions, while the object is the target of these actions. Design ideas ought to explore the psychological possibilities of these relationships. Depending on purpose, design should sometimes emphasize the functional, and at other times, the emotional: if either is completely missing from a work, it cannot be called design.

Shared aesthetic sensibilities are what make all these relationships gel. Design arises from the interdependence of designer, client, user, and the larger society of which they are all a part. Designer and client may agree on a particular *design*, but it is not really design unless it passes muster with users and society as a whole.

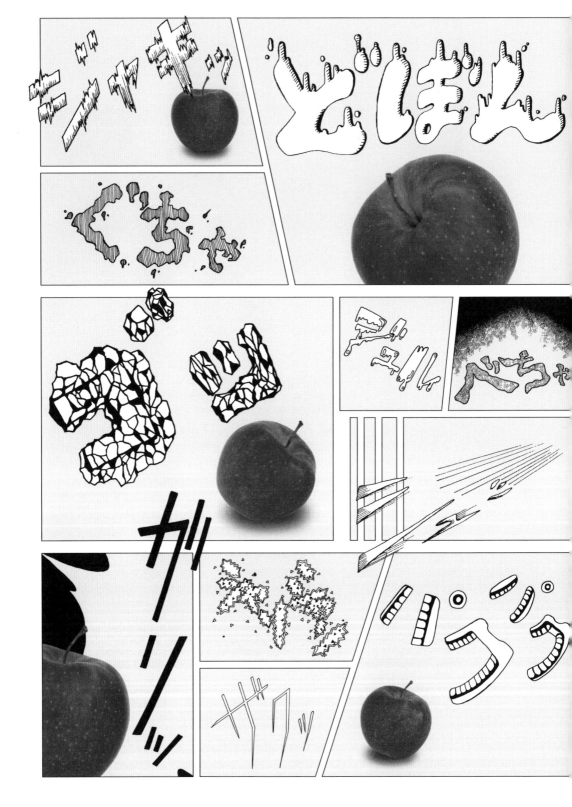

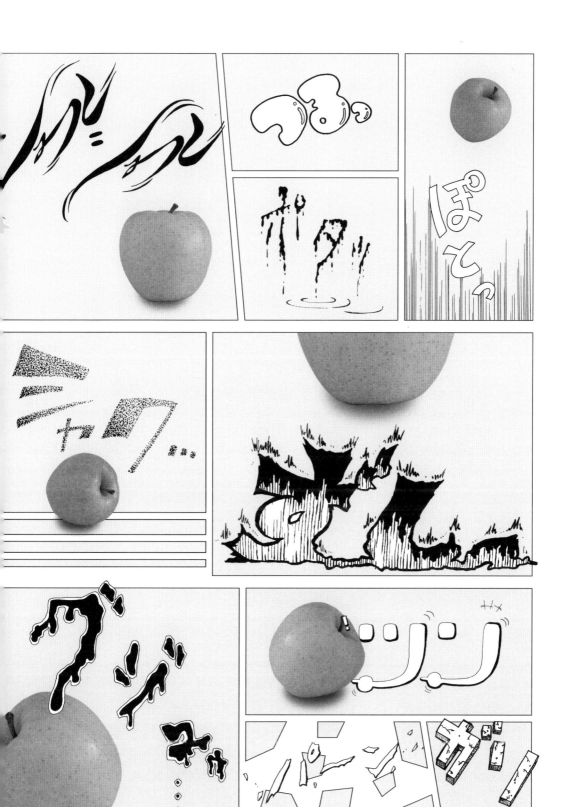

12 | Apple: Thought-Object

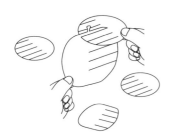

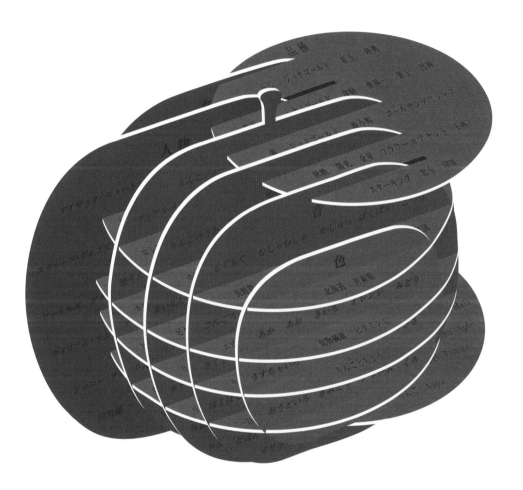

A Three-Dimensional Map of Mental Processes

Looking over the correlation charts created during the apple word-association activity, I noticed that the keywords in each category seemed to link to one another and form a new, larger web of correlations. This new web in turn sparks new word associations, which form still more until the web has become too complex to express in two dimensions. Let us superimpose this image on human society as a whole. The image is of a vast network of freely interconnecting pathways, like the labyrinthine webs formed by train and bus routes, ship routes, aviation flight paths, expressways, roads, and streets. People and things move through this network, shifting routes and selecting modes of transport according to their destinations and objectives, traveling aboveground and underground, on land, sea, and air. This way of planning routes and selecting a means of getting from point A to point B, sometimes at great speed and sometimes at a snail's pace, is similar to the process of editing.

Obviously, human society does not unfold on a flat surface but in three-dimensional space. It is constantly expanding with advances in technology, and starting to cast its net beyond the earth and into outer space. The next class activity entails taking the mental apple map, which has swelled beyond what is expressible in two dimensions, and turning it into an easily apprehended three-dimensional information network. This enables the viewer to grasp relationships between things and phenomena more clearly, and to unearth hidden treasures of meaning.

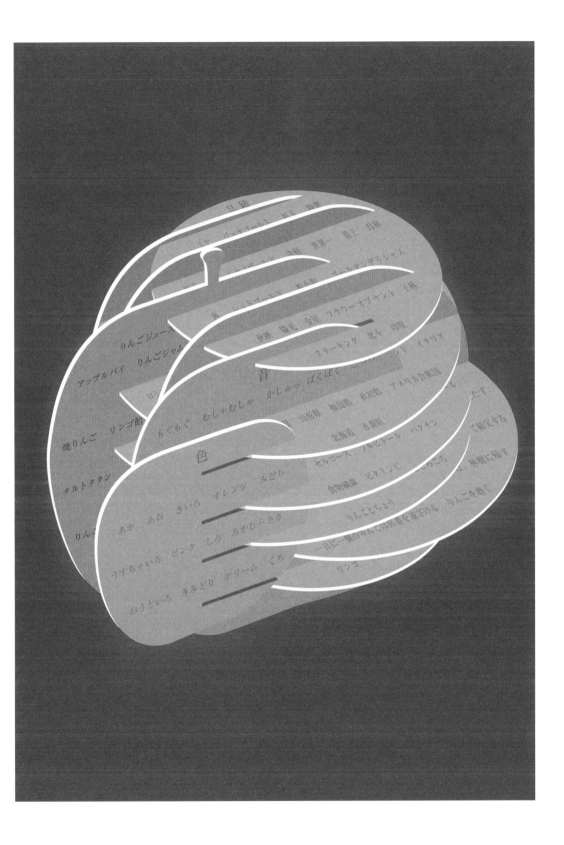

My picture of the birth of a creative concept starts with the pitch-black void of outer space studded with countless stars, discrete specks of memory in the vastness of the brain. One of these points flares brighter when excited by external stimuli, sometimes verbal, sometimes visual. This touches off a chain reaction, with nearby memory-stars in the same constellation of meaning also starting to glow more brightly. Older memories are like more distant stars whose light takes more time to reach us. As we gaze into this firmament, light strikes our eyes and inspires us to make up stories. Then at times there is a sudden flash of inspiration—a shooting star—and we hit upon a concept. A neurologist would no doubt scoff at my naiveté, but each time I see the blaze of a concept across the blackness, I make a wish. These wishes I must keep to myself, as they will not come true if expressed in words. The creation of an apple thought-object, a map of mental processes in three dimensions, is an exercise in visualizing the universe inside the brain.

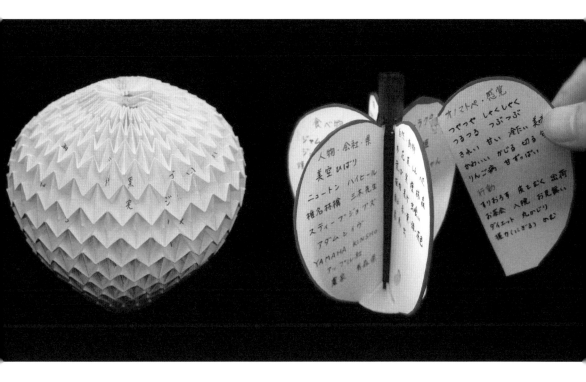

Grasping the Big Picture

I once served as graphic-design director for a large event where many companies were exhibiting. Designing guide signs was an important part of this job, and in preliminary discussions we had difficulty agreeing on how to guide attendees on foot smoothly through the crowded venue during the brief term of the event. The standard procedure would be to distribute maps of the entire space to visitors and position signs throughout the venue that were coordinated with the map. However, this would not give them a swift grasp of the overall space and the relative positions of things.

To address this, I collaborated with the spatial designer to create a knoll overlooking the entire venue, to which attendees were guided upon arrival. On the knoll was a map of the overall venue, and looking at the map while actually viewing the entire space below allowed visitors to grasp the big picture, after which they proceeded to their destinations. If you have ever

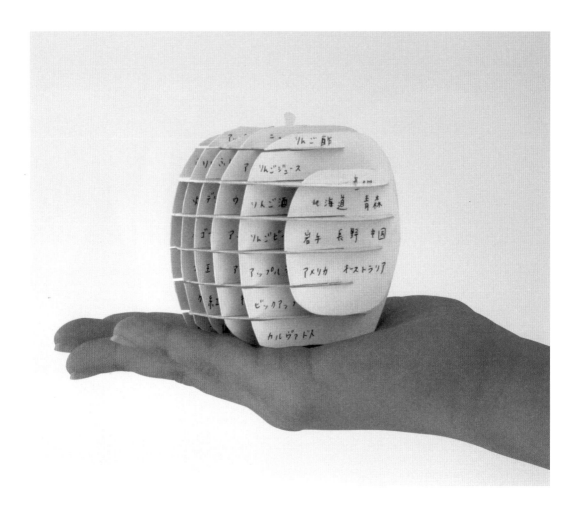

stood in a high place and seen a panoramic view of a city, you know that it generates a map of the city below that the body internalizes, a map that penetrates to the subconscious mind and becomes part of the self. The creation of an apple thought-object is an activity enabling participants to visualize fragments of their internal thoughts in three dimensions. What matters here is to understand the importance of seeing the big picture. This means objectively apprehending the entirety of something and internalizing its structure; and not just getting a bird's-eye view from above but also seeing it from below, front, back, left and right. We must be able to switch information around and edit it at will. Grasping the big picture makes it easy to find your way to your destination.

Meeting with Happy Accidents

In my design studio, there is a rule that bookshelves are not to be organized. This means that it takes some time to find the book you are looking for, but you have wonderful and inspiring chance encounters with other books along the way. It is terribly inefficient to spend large amounts of time just looking up a word in the dictionary, but in the process of hitting on concepts and ideas, efficient procedures are not the rule. Rather, it seems to me that they are the exception, and happy accidents are the rule. Often my brain hums with delighted inspiration at a passage in a book that I was not originally looking for.

The phenomenon of meeting with happy accidents is known as "serendipity," a word coined by the British politician and novelist Horace Walpole. To turn serendipity to our advantage, we must have the ability to find value in things discovered by chance along the way, rather than staying stuck on the thing we are looking for. I keep my bookcases disorganized in order to hone this ability. A lot of Nobel laureates say their discoveries or inventions sprang from happy accidents. Of course not everyone can be a genius, but it is certainly true that intuition, and the brainstorms and awakenings that go with it, are the things we need most in many situations.

The apple thought-object is an assemblage of awakenings, inspired by unexpected meetings with words and other words in seemingly random

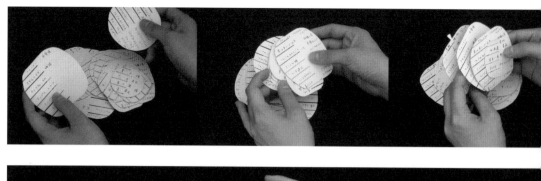

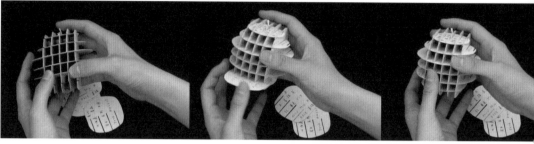

motion. We observe these meetings as we view from every conceivable angle the mental map of words that were inspired freely by the apple and placed into categories. Awakenings are hiding in unexpected places. To find them, you need a wealth of experiences, the memories they generate, and the powers of intuition to connect them.

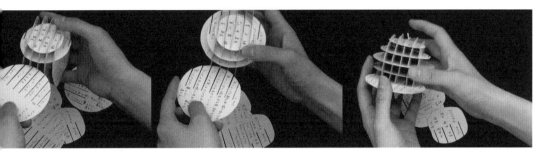

13 | Apple: Flip Book

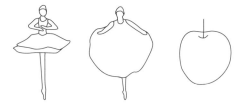

Making a Story

In the single-line picture activity, the students made an illustrated story by connecting five scenes together. You might say they drew pictures for the cover and each chapter of an apple novel that did not have any text. The reader could then look at the pictures and freely imagine any kind of plot. Design is made up of a client and a designer hired to visualize a certain kind of content. But when you design a book, there is also a writer involved. A manga by comparison is drawn and written by one person.

In addition to giving students a chance to enjoy making designs as a team, I also wanted to let them experience the joy and responsibility of being an author. Using texts, pictures, and photos based on their own ideas and thoughts, writers convey a unique way of thinking to society. The content becomes a product and people who like it pay for it.

By making a story with an apple flip-book (essentially the gateway to animation), you can imbue pictures with movement. As you undoubtedly know, a flip book is the fundamental principle behind animation. You draw a series of subtly changing pictures on a bundle of paper like a memo pad, and create movement by simply flipping the pages. Normally, it would be necessary to use twenty-four frames per second to create smooth movement in animation. In this workshop, however, I decided to see what

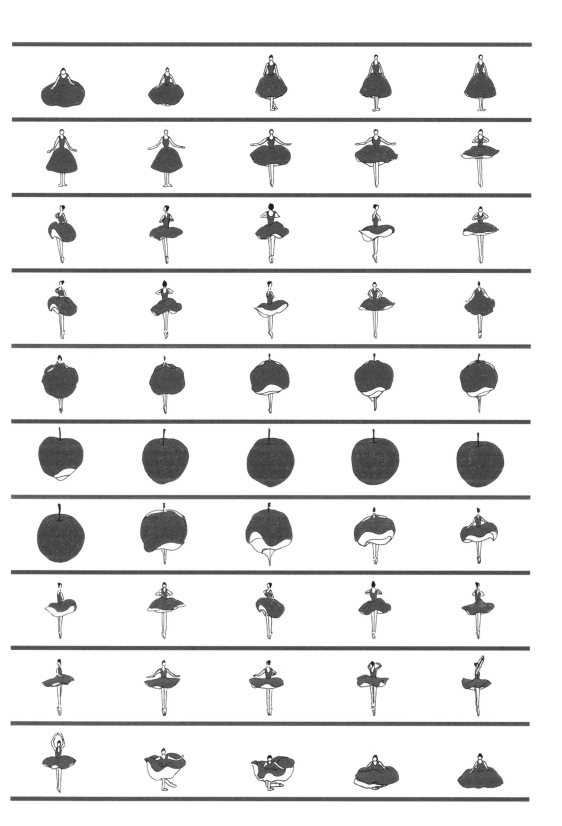

kind of movements the students could make by limiting the number of pages to sixty. It would take less than three seconds to create a smooth movement. They would first have to come up with a movement like a GIF animation that could be expressed in a limited number of frames. Then they would make a short story using only sixty sheets of paper to convey the content in a complete manner with a clear sequence of introduction, development, turn, and conclusion like a four-panel cartoon. When they flipped the pages, the pictures would move in the way that they had intended. A story would emerge as the book began to narrate the event.

Becoming Aware of Time and Space

The rhythm of the flip books varied depending on how fast you flipped the pages, creating subtle differences in space and time. Sometimes the movement looked fluid, sometimes it looked jerky, and sometimes the pages would get stuck in the middle. Striving to realize a smooth movement, many of the students tried over and over again.

Despite using the same set of pictures, the spatial and temporal lag was different each time. This was actually surprisingly interesting. Just as the same script could be expressed very differently depending on the actor, the flow of a story varies according to the director or producer. Here, the lag was simply produced by the way you flipped the pages, but

it functioned to connect the *ma* (gaps). By intentionally staggering the timing, you could make someone laugh or by removing the *ma* in the flow, you could create a lingering memory. The concept of *ma* is essential to Japanese art and culture. The word suggests a spatial void or a temporal standstill. But it is more than just a void or standstill. Part of the all-important flow in noh, kabuki, music, and painting, *ma* is closely related to rhythm and breathing. It was originally a musical concept, but it has since expanded to other fields of art. By creating a lingering sensation or leaving a blank, you can prompt a variety of interpretations and enhance someone's imagination. In this case, an absence indicates something important in the overall expression. *Ma* is not a break in the concept of time, but rather the act of bringing time to life. Seeing *ma* as a generative element causes something to start wriggling around.

By making the flip books, the students became aware of *ma*. There is not anything there, but we somehow seem to hear a breath of life rise out of this creative process. The *ma* in the apple might be seen as a space that produces a kind of relationship. The *kanji* character for *ma* is combined with other characters to create the Japanese words for "space," "time," and "human being," and the flip books, by altering the *ma* that connects people and time, emerge from between the *ma*.

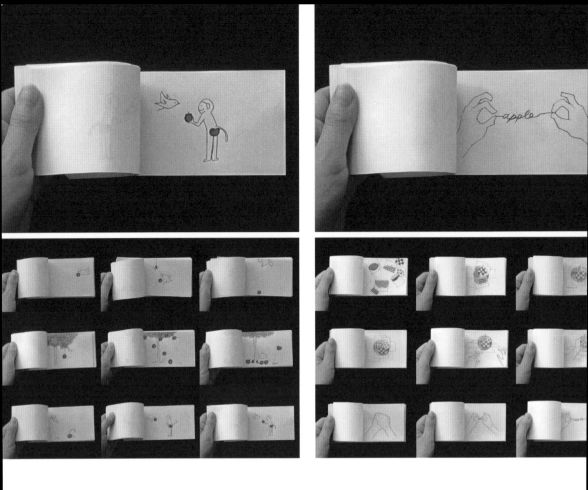

Breathing Life into a Picture

The two-dimensional pictures began to move. A collection of unique movements and ideas were realized in the form of a super-short animated work. By adding music, it was amazing to see how the pictures took on a life of their own. This sense of life is undoubtedly what excited people like Osamu Tezuka, Hayao Miyazaki, and Walt Disney. The alter ego you draw suddenly starts walking, dancing, and talking. There is not anyone who would not feel excited at the thought.

What is important now is the content of the story. Captivated by the movement, we tend to neglect the story. Considering what to convey to the viewer leads to an emotional or sympathetic response. Artistic

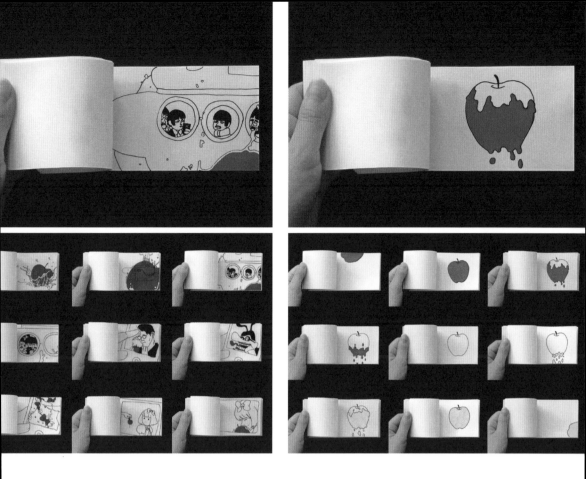

expression is not limited to pictures. Whether it is photographs or typography, it is crucial to convey your intentions. Design cannot be cultivated in a place without ideas. Seeing her pictures start to move, one student said, "It is like a child of your own!" Many of the others nodded in agreement. She was right: design is the child of an idea.

14 | Apple: Textbook

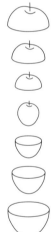

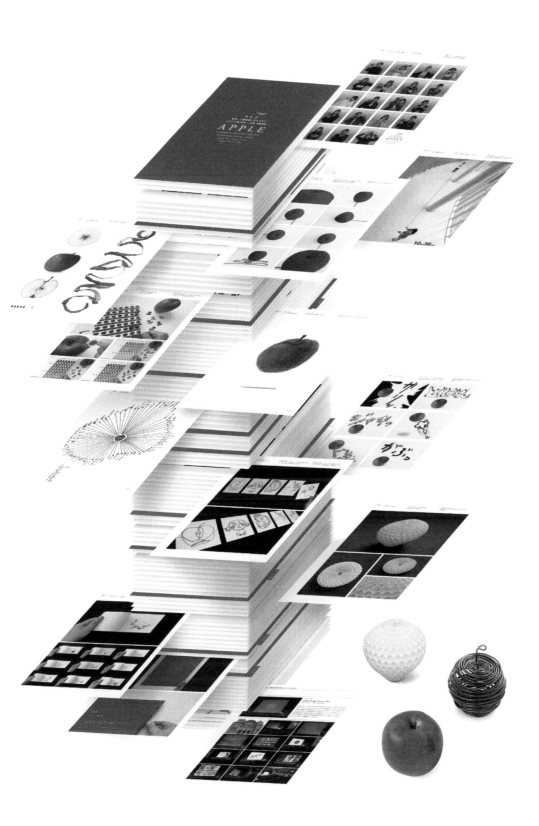

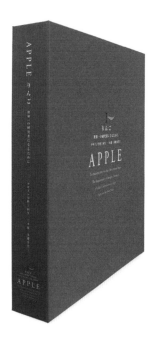

Making a Textbook

To teach freshmen majoring in design some basic practices, I came up with a new type of class by designing a way of learning. I set out to create a course in which every lesson would contain some kind of "realization" and the "thrill of learning," inspiring a greater interest in design as the class went along. On the first day of class, I burned some incense in the orientation room to create an atmosphere that was different from that of any other classroom through the presence of a fragrance. I wanted to make an invisible building there out of the fragrance, and also to convey the idea that there is always more than meets the eye. And most of all, I wanted to use the sense of smell to communicate the importance of designing a situation prior to the emergence of an actual form. I would like to continue discussing the nature of concepts while making reference to these values of visible and invisible design.

A concept is an idea. And "conception" has a similar meaning, but it is more concrete and personal than "concept," and focuses on the process of shaping a concept. The word "conception" also means "pregnancy." Let us

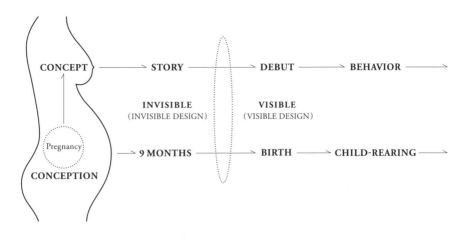

CONCEPT	→ STORY	→ DEBUT	→ BEHAVIOR →
	INVISIBLE (INVISIBLE DESIGN)	VISIBLE (VISIBLE DESIGN)	
Pregnancy	→ 9 MONTHS	→ BIRTH	→ CHILD-REARING →
CONCEPTION			

compare the two a bit more. Please think of conception as an "invisible life" that remains within a woman's body until it is born, and the maturation process that occurs after the baby is born as a "visible life." Actually, between the time that a woman becomes pregnant and the baby was born, this life continues to mature as a fetus. And since we can use ultrasound and other techniques to visualize the shape of the fetus, it is not strictly correct to refer to it as an "invisible life." If we translate the formula that begins with conception or pregnancy (invisible life) and leads to birth and later child-rearing (visible life) into design terms, we might say that a concept or idea (invisible design) leads to creation and later activity (visible design). If we use a diagram to compare the birth of a child and the creation of a design, we see that neither is an end in itself. It is necessary to arrive at a sustainable plan for the future. Further, it is deeply significant to experience the entire process that begins with an invisible life or design and concludes with a visible life or design. The importance of a principle or concept hinges on the act of living in relation to society.

I have documented the entire apple course. I explained the educational principles and concepts I have devised for each activity using an index

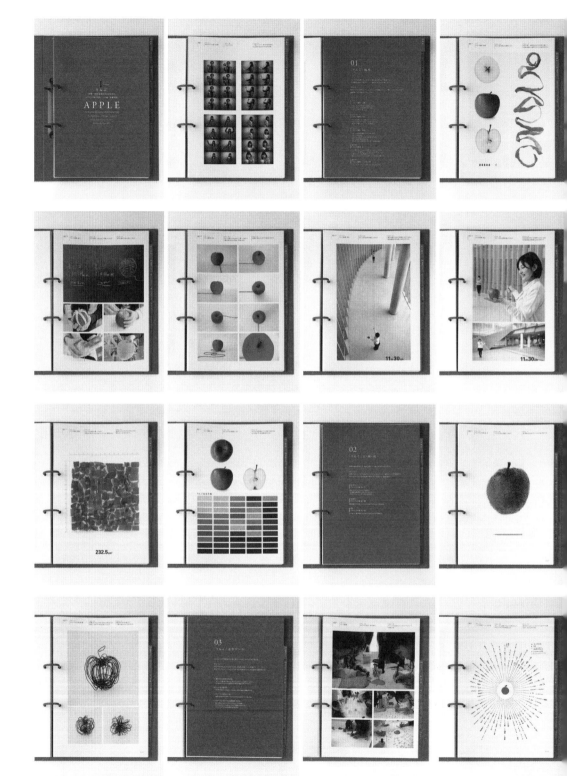

format and have divided them into easy-to-understand chapters. Then I selected photographs from a total of nearly four hundred pictures that were taken throughout the course to convey the actual conditions in the classroom. This includes works by each student and an abridged version of all of the works made in the class. This allows the students to continually review their files, which gradually increase in size each week. In form, the files are similar to yearbooks, inspiring fond and nostalgic memories. And after all of the apple activities are finished, the students have a file of documents that recalls a textbook. Created by everyone, the new book's style conveys the thrill of learning. This is the concept I strove to achieve.

Looking Back at the Course

The students bring their files with them to every class. They use them to store handouts and their own works, and they often open their files when they have a spare moment during the class. Whether they are reviewing something from a few weeks back, or connecting the words they assembled in the word-association game to the next idea, the students use

the files much more than I had originally expected. Some of them show their files to their family and friends to help explain the appearance and content of the class. Surprisingly, it also seems that the files, which the students have played a central role in creating, increase their recollections. Richard Saul Wurman, a recognized master of "understanding," stresses that the key to making something complex seem clear is comprehensible design. This means clarity rather than simplicity.

And this is what Wurman says about understanding. He suggests that if you really want to see if you understand a book, try explaining it to someone else. If the person says, "I see!", you know that you have understood it. It might sound like a simple dialogue, but the point is that you reach an understanding by providing a lucid explanation in your own words of what you experienced through your senses. When students try to explain this course to their family and friends, it is most effective for them to use their files and revisit past classes. "Understanding" is the gateway to everything. At times, we become a bit faint-hearted when facing the future. We also tend to be constrained by an attachment to the past. In reflecting on the class, students do not merely gaze back at what has already occurred, but slowly digest each piece of the apple workshops. Then the ingredients of design begin to seep out. This is what it means to become aware. In other words, looking back involves savoring your experiences and giving your realizations a physical form through your own words and expressions.

Sharing the Process

The Japanese word *kyoiku*, meaning "education," is made up of two *kanji* characters. The first means "teaching," and the second "raising." After accepting this job as a teacher, I wondered what I could do. Of course, straight teaching would have been one option, but I decided to place a greater emphasis on coaching, and saw my role as someone who could help enhance my students' way of thinking. I conceived of my job as a shift from teaching to coaching and ultimately to raising young people.

As the owner of my own design firm as well an art director and graphic designer, I am constantly talking to my young staff about design, and assembling a team for each project. Our work is the practice and study of

design. By accepting this teaching post, I added a new activity to my daily routine. Now I essentially wear two hats: designer at Ken Miki & Associates and educator at the university. Although this has become part of my daily reality, I am still not quite dexterous enough to smoothly shift between the two. As a result, it seemed natural that if I integrated teaching with my other projects, I could provide students with practical learning that was more than just a desk theory. By documenting these activities, it would be possible to capture and understand the study and growth process. This would also make the project socially viable as a form of open education. Through my teaching job, I came to realize the meaning of this project. I shared all of the teaching, coaching, and raising processes with my students, and then I shared them with the public. Posting my apple lectures on YouTube* and creating this book are all part of this process. Each time I taught a class, it was clear that the students' awareness of design was undergoing a rapid change. My eyes were practically blinded with excitement as I watched these young creative minds sprout like buds.

*http://www.youtube.com/watch?v=I-5noogmZmo

15 | Apple: Conclusion

Learning to Design, Designing to Learn

APPLE
Ken Miki

Design Philosophy

Why an apple?

Apples played a central role in many inventions, discoveries, and creations throughout history.

1. The forbidden fruit eaten by Adam and Eve
2. Isaac Newton's discovery of the law of universal gravitation
3. The record company run by the Beatles
4. The company that Steve Jobs used to launch a computer revolution

[English]
delicious

[word origin]
いし（美し）
good, pleasant, splendid, clever, tasty

Japanese ideograms
美味しい

おいしい　=　いしい（美し）

美 | 味

美意識
sense of beauty

意味
concept

appreciate
discern → understand
recognize → observe
perceive → learn

In ancient Greek, "love" (*philos*) + "knowledge" (*sophia*)
"love of knowledge" (philosophia)
学問 = learning
聞いを学ぶ = to learn questions

What does it mean to think, make, convey, and learn?

What does it mean to think?

five senses
1. seeing
2. hearing
3. feeling
4. smelling
5. tasting

What does it mean to make?

What does it mean to convey?

What does it mean to learn?

→ design ←

Awareness

Intelligence

Sensibility

Revision
Visualization
Analysis
Understanding
Imagination
Observation

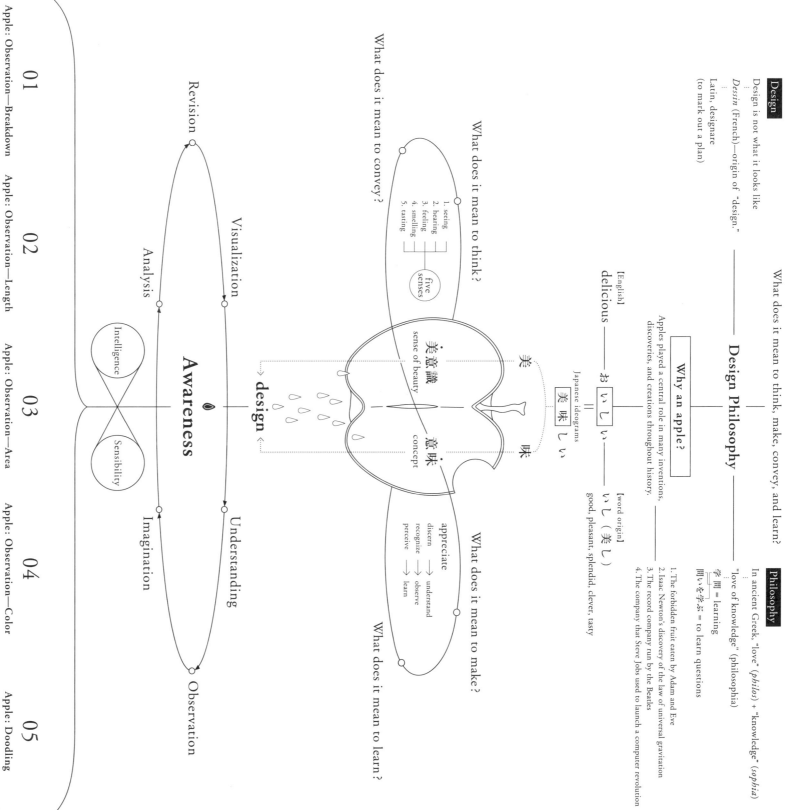

Design

Design is not what it looks like

Dessin (French)—origin of "design."

Latin, designare
(to mark out a plan)

01 Apple: Observation—Breakdown

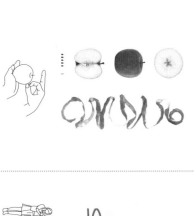

- The Fruit You Thought You Knew
- I Saw the Same Thing, But It Was Different
- Becoming the World's Greatest

02 Apple: Observation—Length

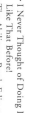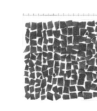

- Subtracting Information
- A Fusion of Functional Beauty and Emotional Beauty
- Transience, Sorrow, and Gallantry
- Designing Everything, Down to

03 Apple: Observation—Area

- I Never Thought of Doing It Like That Before!
- The Ability to Read, Edit, and Redraw a Map
- Erasing the Name

04 Apple: Observation—Color

- Colors Speak to Us
- Freeing and Sharing Colors
- Does a Rainbow Really Have

05 Apple: Doodling

- The Search for Hidden Meanings
- Speaking Design and Listening Design

Osaka Design Forum 2012
Organized by Osaka University of Arts at the Osaka Central Public Hall

Understanding
(Often Overlooked)

Limited by preconceptions and prejudices, many of us fail to correctly identify the reasons, causes, and significance of the matter at hand. We have a vague notion of something without thoroughly understanding it. Or more to the point, many of us do not realize that we do not understand. Understanding is the key to everything.

Observation
(Thinking That You Know Is the Most Dangerous Thing)

Search for the source, determine relationships, and accumulate facts. This is what it means to observe.

Imagination
(Build Up a Hypothesis)

Derive a concept from this information, and begin to construct an idea in three dimensions as if you were erecting a building based on your objectives. In this "imaginative" act, you can build up a hypothesis.

Analysis
(Restructuring)

It is vital to find a necessity in the concept that links the subject to your objectives. Once the necessity becomes clear, you have to "analyze" it. Unless

Open Education

06 Apple: Points

· Think Big, Act Small
· Learning from Limitations
· Bringing a Still Life to Life
· CMY Pointillism

07 Apple: Line

· Thinking with the Hands
· An Aerial Apple
· Writhing Perseverance

08 Apple: Word-association Game

· Brain-borrowing
· Apple Correlation Charts

09 Apple: Party

· Communication, Hospitality, and Art
· Apples and Me

10 Apple: One Line

· Connecting, Expanding, Discovering
· Simplification Accentuates Structure
· Design, Environment, and Psychology

11 Apple: Onomatopoeia

· Wordless Words
· Learning by Imitation
· Design Resides in Relationships Between Subject and Object

12 Apple: Thought-Object

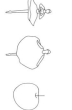

· A Three-Dimensional Map of Mental Processes
· Grasping the Big Picture
· Meeting with Happy Accidents

13 Apple: Flip Book

· Making a Story
· Becoming Aware of Time and Space
· Breathing Life into a Picture

14 Apple: Textbook

· Making a Textbook
· Looking Back at the Course
· Sharing the Process

15 Apple: Conclusion

· Understanding—Observation
· Imagination—Analysis—Revision
· Visualization—Becoming Aware

Design Quality

Consumers — Creators — Clients

Fulfilling life

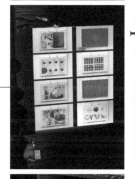

For those who are studying design for the first time,
those who have been involved with design for many years,
those who are teaching design, and those who have no interest in design

you have the courage to analyze and restructure your plan, you will simply continue to move forward without taking note of various disparities that have arisen.

Revision
(Verbalization)

This involves deriving a concept based on a unique perspective, defining clear content, and determining a course of activity. All of the principles and concepts needed to take concrete action are now in place.

Visualization
(Putting a Principle in Action)

It is sometimes said that design is the act of expressing a principle in an easy-to-understand and original way. We might then see design as a child born of principle.

Becoming Aware

Each of these steps helps us attain an awareness of new values and ideas. It is this process that gives birth to design.

What Is Learning?

The word "philosophy" is derived from the Greek *philosophia*, a term formed by connecting the word for "love" (*philos*) and the word for "knowledge" (*sophia*). As you might expect, *philosophia* suggests a "love of knowledge" and was used in ancient Greece to refer to learning as a whole. This workshop-style apple course was based on the design philosophy of searching for the origins of various ways of thinking and making, and remained focused on discovering the true essence of design. This was an incredibly important part of the course's content.

If you reverse the *kanji* characters used to write *gakumon* (learning), you end up with the phrase, "to study questions." I believe that at the heart of learning is the desire to continually question, thirst for information, and ask why and how. In this course, I attached special importance to the idea of "learning to learn." And by incorporating the notion that the world will open up by persistently pursuing one subject, I added the subtitle, "Becoming the World's Greatest Researcher."

Every activity in the apple course was based on the concept of becoming aware. For example, one activity dealt with observing the apple physically and realizing that you did not really know as much about apples as you thought. Or in another activity, by making a book of color samples, the students realized that everything that has been marketed as a product was designed by someone, and that if you cannot find what you are looking for, whether it be a color, a word, or paper, you can devise a way to make it. In the onomatopoeia typography activity, students realized that they could feel design by taking the words for sounds and noises that appeared in manga and seeing them as physical letters that express emotions. There was also an activity in which they realized that they could discover a diverse range of expressive methods through the use of rules and limitations; and in another one, involving the apple word-association game, they realized that editing helps us discover categories and contents. Also, by using the method of "brain-borrowing" to adopt other people's ideas and values, the students honed their sense of serendipity (the ability to encounter happy accidents) through influence and excitement. Serendipity is the ability to discover completely unexpected things to enhance your ideas. By keeping your antennae up in daily life, you can expand the potential for realization by making your ideas more flexible. This course was made up of activities in which awareness functioned as a powerful motivating force behind a concept. Everything was intended to provide experiences for those studying design for the first time, those with no interest in design, those involved with design for many years, and those teaching design.

All of the students strove to find a true motivation and serious attitude, and I constantly tried to provide them with well-timed opportunities to display their abilities. Each person has a distinct personality. The most important objective of this course is to develop an awareness that will help students freely express their individuality. I wondered if it would be possible to visualize an invisible philosophy (or love of knowledge) through this series of workshops. And I searched for a new type of teaching and a new type of textbook to create an overall course that would inspire the students to find their true intentions. My educational policy is that a teacher must never try to create copies of himself. On the other hand, as suggested by the phrase "to learn is to imitate," it is also important to understand the significance of the oral tradition in learning. In the end, I did not worry too much about whether my students copied me or not. The most vital thing is not how much you know, but rather to take the humble attitude that there are still many things you do not know, and to take an interest in learning more. The genuine desire to understand and to be taught enhances our ability to learn. When I accepted this job, I was very worried about what I could teach these young students of eighteen or nineteen as they prepared to cross the threshold of design.

I myself frequently consider the essential nature of design. As a young person, I abandoned my studies due to adolescent worries and set out on the road to design. I bet my life on design and aspired to learn. The feeling that I had not studied enough and needed to learn more is what drove me to become the person I am today. Learning demands that we search for our own subject. *Apple* is a study platform that provides a venue for realizing, learning, and gathering; it is supported by the students' desire to learn.

Learning begins with a love of knowledge.

Afterword

The Osaka Design Forum, organized by Osaka University of Arts, attracted an audience of close to eight hundred people when it was held at the Osaka Central Public Hall on May 20, 2012. In order to transmit Osaka design culture, several guests are invited to speak at the event each year. Toshiyuki Kita, a product designer and head of the university's design department, asked me to give a presentation at the forum just prior to the apple course. I struggled for a while before deciding on a topic, but since the event was sponsored by the university and I was a newly-appointed teacher and designer, I eventually settled on "learning and design." I thought that by using documents related to the apple course, the concept of which I had already begun to refine, I could explain my educational principles and practices. Thinking back now, this must have been around the time that I was trying to gauge my staff's reactions to the apple concept and before I had any idea how the students would respond and what kind of work would emerge as a result.

After I started the course, however, my worries were quickly dispelled. And as the course progressed, the classroom became filled with feverish enthusiasm. The students' passion grew ever more intense as their files thickened. As the date of my talk approached, the office fell into a state of utter confusion as I tried to take care of my regular duties as well as preparing for the university course, making files, and creating slides for my talk. Preparations were moving forward at exactly the same time as I was trying to document the students' progress in the class. Just prior to the talk, I rushed to prepare my slides and arrived at the forum after only just having had a chance to review the entire presentation.

The audience was made up of a wide variety of people, including students from Osaka University of Arts and other universities, professional designers, and the general public. I had settled on the basic theme of discovering the essence of design. In order to convey my message in the most comprehensible manner, I began by explaining the close connection between design and daily life using four subjects that have been familiar to everyone since elementary school: mathematics, Japanese, social studies, and science. I wanted to stress that there was more to design than color and shape. Then I used my minutely detailed record of the apple course to explain the same content that I have outlined in this book.

My presentation was much more well received than I had expected, and I was in turn asked to speak at several other universities and companies. This included a request from the faculty development department of a certain university to speak to a group of teachers. This led to a request from the Alliance Graphique Internationale (AGI) to deliver a speech abroad. Every year the AGI, an organization made up of world-renowned designers selected by a review board, holds a design conference, featuring lectures and other events, in a different city. Members from all over the world attend the event. In 2012, it was held in

Hong Kong, and I presented my apple talk to the top international designers. As I am not very good at English, I relied on an interpreter and prepared some slides with English captions. More than anything, I wanted to express my message in my own voice. It was a bit nerve-wracking to face a roomful of so many people I admired.

Among the audience was Lars Müller, the current international president of the AGI. After my talk, he mentioned my presentation in his greeting to the group after assuming the post of president: "The AGI's work includes supporting all types of activities to help educate and assist promising young graphic designers. Ken Miki's apple course should be commended as one example of such activities." I was surprised, or more to the point, I was deeply moved. A few months later, I received an offer from Lars Müller Publishers to write this book. As it happened, the company has published many books that I treasure, so it was a great honor to have *Apple* added to its catalogue. It was like a dream to think that the educational method I had conceived of only a year and several months earlier would be published abroad. During a visit to Japan, Müller offered me some advice on writing an insightful text. I was worried about whether or not readers would be able to understand my clumsy writing, but I somehow managed to finish the book.

I would like to express my sincere gratitude to Lars Müller for listening to my presentation at the AGI conference, visiting my office while he was in Japan, and agreeing to publish this book.

I would also like to take this opportunity to thank Toshiyuki Kita, who suggested that I accept a teaching post at the university and invited me to speak at the Osaka Design Forum. It was due to his efforts that I was able to realize the apple course and presentation.

In addition, I would like to thank the translator and editor Christopher Stephens for his hard work in translating this book. To understand a writer's ideas and translate them into an appropriate expression in another language requires a literary sensibility and capability that extends far beyond merely substituting one word for another. I imagine it was particularly difficult to translate the chapter on onomatopoeia.

I would also like to extend my gratitude to Toshihiko Murakami for taking the photographs used in this publication; and also to my revered teacher, the graphic designer Tetsuo Katayama, who taught me the ABCs of design. My experiences as a student have proven to be extremely useful in my current role as a teacher of the next generation of designers. I would also like to offer my deepest sympathies to Katayama's family following the death in Boston in January 2013 of his older brother

Toshihiro Katayama, who taught at Harvard University for many years and provided me with guidance whenever he returned to Japan.

I would also like to express my appreciation to my staff who spent a tremendous amount of time helping me prepare the apple course and assisting me with the design of this book. Beginning with the apple party, the entire staff has supported me in this project.

In addition, I would like to express my gratitude to my wife Tomoko for allowing me to write on my days off and go into the office to work on this book. Without her understanding, I would never have completed it.

In closing, I should also say that without the passion and ingenuity of the Team Miki students, I would never have been able to create either the apple course or the textbook. And of course, they were also an essential element of this book. I would like to send out my sincere regards and dedicate this book to all of them.

Ken Miki

Born in Kobe in 1955.
Established Ken Miki & Associates in 1982.

Miki has developed a narrative-based approach to design through "speaking design," in which he advances a design in a manner that is similar to speaking, and "listening design," in which he searches for the fundaments of a given thing. Contained within his quiet expressions, based on the theme of "becoming aware of awareness," is an emotional form of communication.

He has received numerous awards including the Japan Graphic Designers Association New Designer Award, Japan Typography Association Grand Prize, International Poster Triennial in Toyama 2006 Silver Prize, and the NY ADC Distinctive Merit Award.

Among his most notable works are the congress kit for the World Design Congress, a promotion for IBM Japan ThinkPad i Series, and various projects for Belle Maison, Keikyu Department Store, and Osaka University of Pharmaceutical Sciences.

He has given presentations at countless events both in Japan and abroad, including the Business of Design Week 2009 (Hong Kong), Game Developers Conference 2009 (China), Agideas International Design Week 2011 (Australia), and Alliance Graphique Internationale 2012 (Hong Kong).

He is a member of the Alliance Graphique Internationale (AGI), Japan Graphic Designers Association (JAGDA), and Tokyo Typedirectors Club (TDC). He also currently works as a professor at Osaka University of Arts.

www.ken-miki.net

APPLE

Learning to Design, Designing to Learn

Author	Ken Miki
Editorial concept	Ken Miki, Lars Müller
Translation	Christopher Stephens
Editing and design	Ken Miki, Masahiko Setoyama, Yoko Inuyama, Akira Ono
Photography	Toshihiko Murakami, Ken Miki
Printing and binding	Kösel, Altusried-Krugzell, Germany

© 2014 Lars Müller Publishers, Zürich

Lars Müller Publishers
Zürich, Switzerland
www.lars-mueller-publishers.com

ISBN 978-3-03778-386-3

Printed in Germany